TAYLOR SWIFT
UKULELE COLLECTION

Cover photo by Larry Busacca/Getty Images

ISBN 978-1-70513-554-9

HAL•LEONARD®

Visit Hal Leonard Online at
www.halleonard.com

Contact us:
Hal Leonard
7777 West Bluemound Road
Milwaukee, WI 53213
Email: info@halleonard.com

In Europe, contact:
Hal Leonard Europe Limited
42 Wigmore Street
Marylebone, London, W1U 2RN
Email: info@halleonardeurope.com

In Australia, contact:
Hal Leonard Australia Pty. Ltd.
4 Lentara Court
Cheltenham, Victoria, 3192 Australia
Email: info@halleonard.com.au

Back to December

Words and Music by Taylor Swift

First note

Verse
Moderately, in 2

1. I'm so glad you made time to see me. How's life?
2. *See additional lyrics*

Tell me, how's your fam - 'ly? I have - n't seen them in a while.

You've been good,

bus - i - er than ev - er. Small talk, work and the weath - er.

Your guard is up and I know why.

noth-in' but miss-in' you, wish-in' that I re-al-ized what I had ___ when you ___

___ were mine. ___ I ___ go back to De-cem-ber, turn ___

___ a-round and make it al - right. I ___ go

back to De-cem-ber all ___ the time. ___

1.
2.

Bridge

I miss ___ your tan skin, ___ your

sweet smile, ___ so good to me, ___ so right; and how you held ___

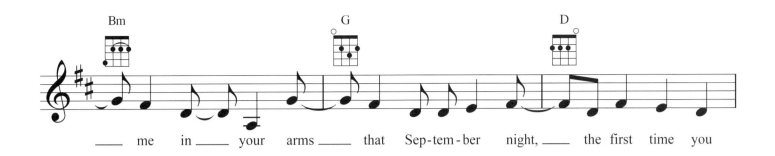

_____ me in _____ your arms _____ that Sep-tem-ber night, _____ the first time you

ev - er saw _____ me cry. _____ May - be this is wish - ful think - in',

prob - a - bly mind - less dream - in'. If we loved a - gain, _____

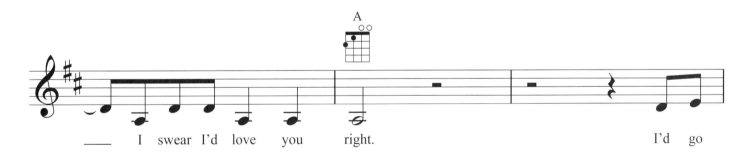

_____ I swear I'd love you right. I'd go

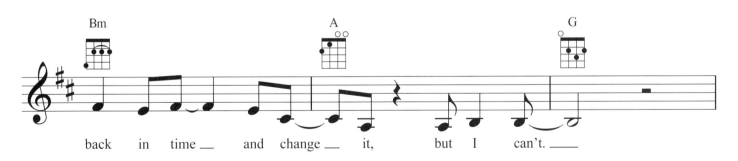

back in time _____ and change _____ it, but I can't. _____

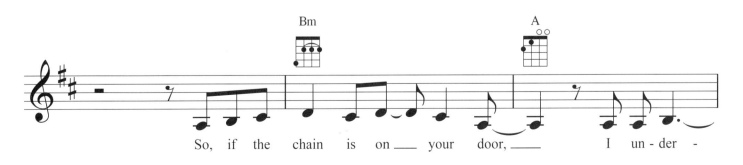

So, if the chain is on _____ your door, _____ I un - der -

Additional Lyrics

2. These days I haven't been sleepin';
   Stayin' up, playin' back myself leavin',
   When your birthday passed and I didn't call.
   Then I think about summer, all the beautiful times
   I watched you laughin' from the passenger side
   And realized I love you in the fall.
   And then the cold came, the dark days when fear crept into my mind.
   You gave me all your love and all I gave you was goodbye.

Bad Blood

Words and Music by Taylor Swift, Max Martin and Shellback

First note

Chorus
Moderately, in 2

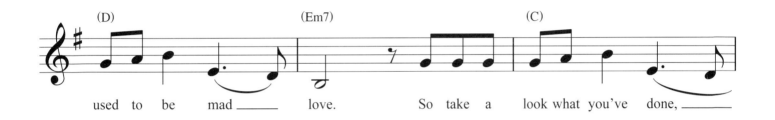

'Cause, ba - by, now we got bad _____ blood. You know, it

used to be mad _____ love. So take a look what you've done, _____

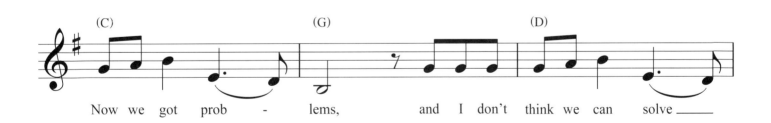

'cause, ba - by, now we got bad _____ blood. Hey!

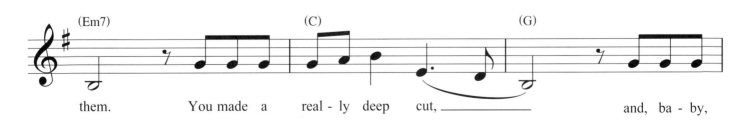

Now we got prob - lems, and I don't think we can solve _____

them. You made a real - ly deep cut, _____ and, ba - by,

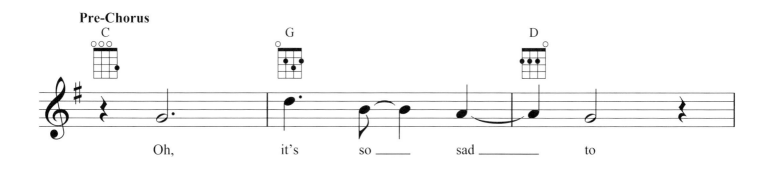

Pre-Chorus

Oh, it's so ___ sad ___ to

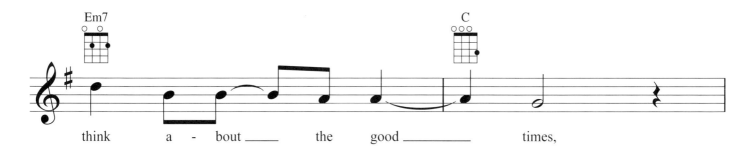

think a - bout ___ the good ___ times,

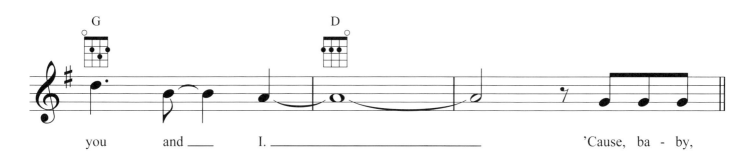

you and ___ I. _____ 'Cause, ba - by,

Chorus

now we got bad ___ blood. You know it used to be mad ___

love. So take a look what you've done, _____ 'cause, ba - by,

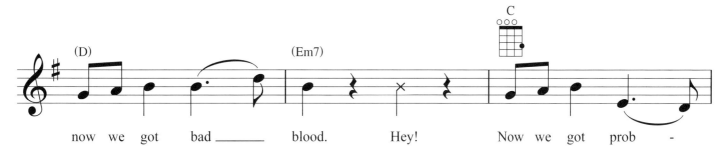

now we got bad ___ blood. Hey! Now we got prob -

Blank Space

Words and Music by Taylor Swift, Max Martin and Shellback

1. Nice to meet you; where you been? I could show _ you in-cred-i-ble
2. Cher-ry lips, _ crys-tal skies; I could show _ you in-cred-i-ble

things: _ mag-ic, mad-ness, heav-en, sin. Saw you there _ and I _____ thought,
things: _ sto-len kiss-es, pret-ty lies. You're the king, _ ba-by, I'm your

"Oh my God, look at that face! You look like my next mis-take.
queen. Find out what you want, be that girl for a month.

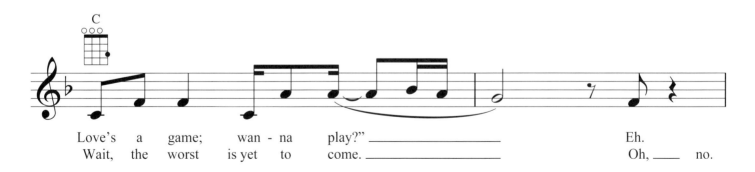

Love's a game; wan-na play?" _____ Eh.
Wait, the worst is yet to come. _____ Oh, ___ no.

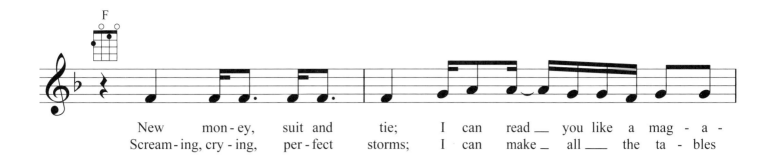

New mon-ey, suit and tie; I can read ___ you like a mag-a-
Scream-ing, cry-ing, per-fect storms; I can make ___ all ___ the ta-bles

zine. ___ Ain't it fun-ny? Ru-mors fly, and I know ___ you heard ___ a-bout
turn. ___ Rose ___ gar-den filled with thorns; keep you sec-ond-guess-ing like,

me. So hey, let's be friends. I'm dy-ing to see how this one ends.
"Oh, my God, who is she?" I ___ get drunk on jeal-ous-y. But

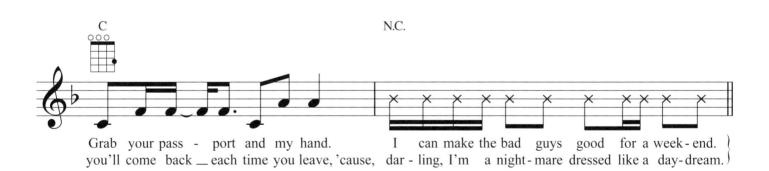

Grab your pass-port and my hand. I can make the bad guys good for a week-end.
you'll come back ___ each time you leave, 'cause, dar-ling, I'm a night-mare dressed like a day-dream.

𝄋 Chorus

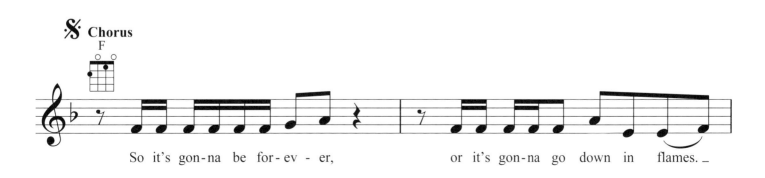

So it's gon-na be for-ev-er, or it's gon-na go down in flames. ___

Dm
You can tell me when it's o - ver, mm, if the high was worth the pain. __

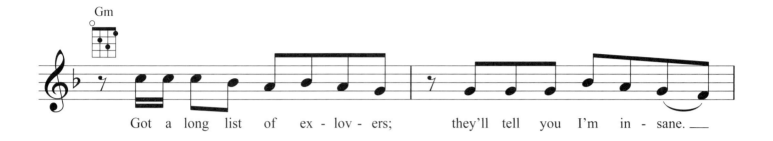

Gm
Got a long list of ex - lov - ers; they'll tell you I'm in - sane. __

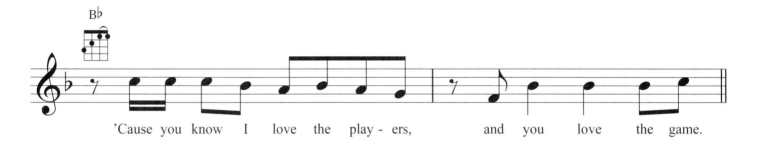

B♭
'Cause you know I love the play - ers, and you love the game.

Chorus

F
'Cause we're young and we're reck - less, we'll take this way too far. __

Dm
It - 'll leave you breath - less, mm, or with a nas - ty scar. __

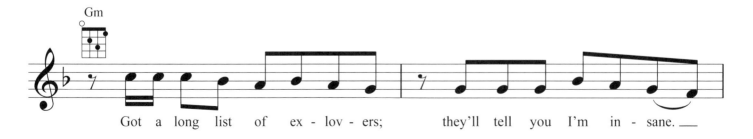

Gm
Got a long list of ex - lov - ers; they'll tell you I'm in - sane. __

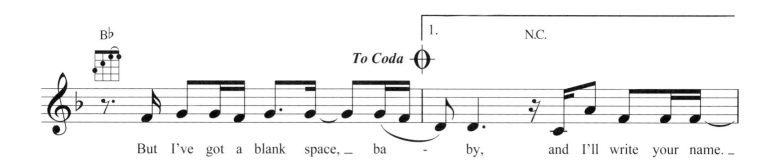

But I've got a blank space, __ ba - by, and I'll write your name. __

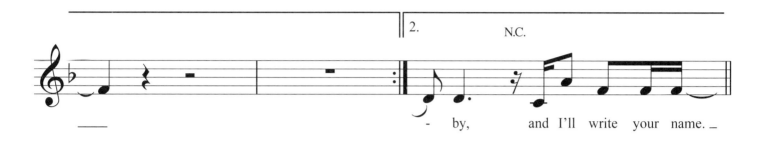

__ - by, and I'll write your name. __

Bridge

__ Boys on - ly want love if it's tor - ture. Don't say I did - n't,

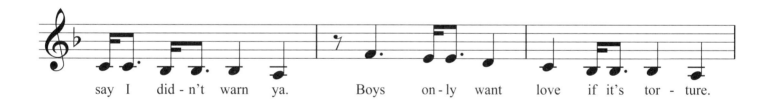

say I did - n't warn ya. Boys on - ly want love if it's tor - ture.

Don't say I did - n't, say I did - n't warn ya.

__ - by, and I'll write your name. __

Cardigan

Words and Music by Taylor Swift and Aaron Dessner

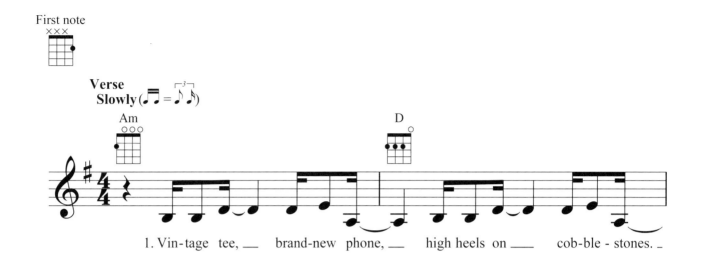

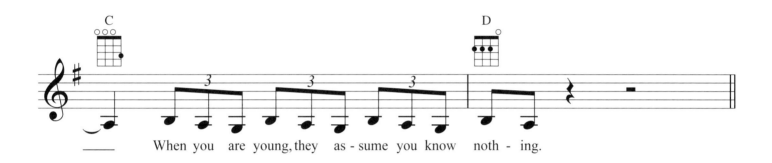

1. Vin-tage tee, __ brand-new phone, __ high heels on __ cob-ble - stones. __
___ When you are young, they as - sume you know noth - ing.

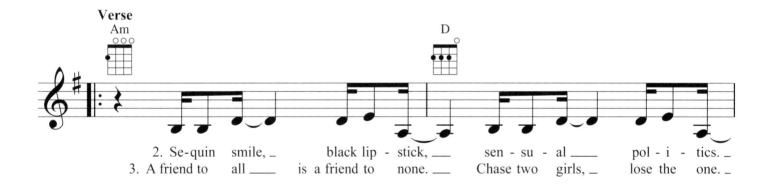

2. Se-quin smile, _ black lip - stick, __ sen - su - al __ pol - i - tics. __
3. A friend to all __ is a friend to none. __ Chase two girls, _ lose the one. __

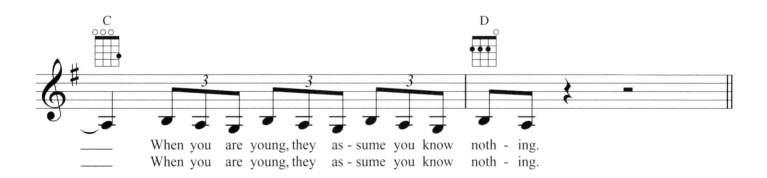

___ When you are young, they as - sume you know noth - ing.
___ When you are young, they as - sume you know noth - ing.

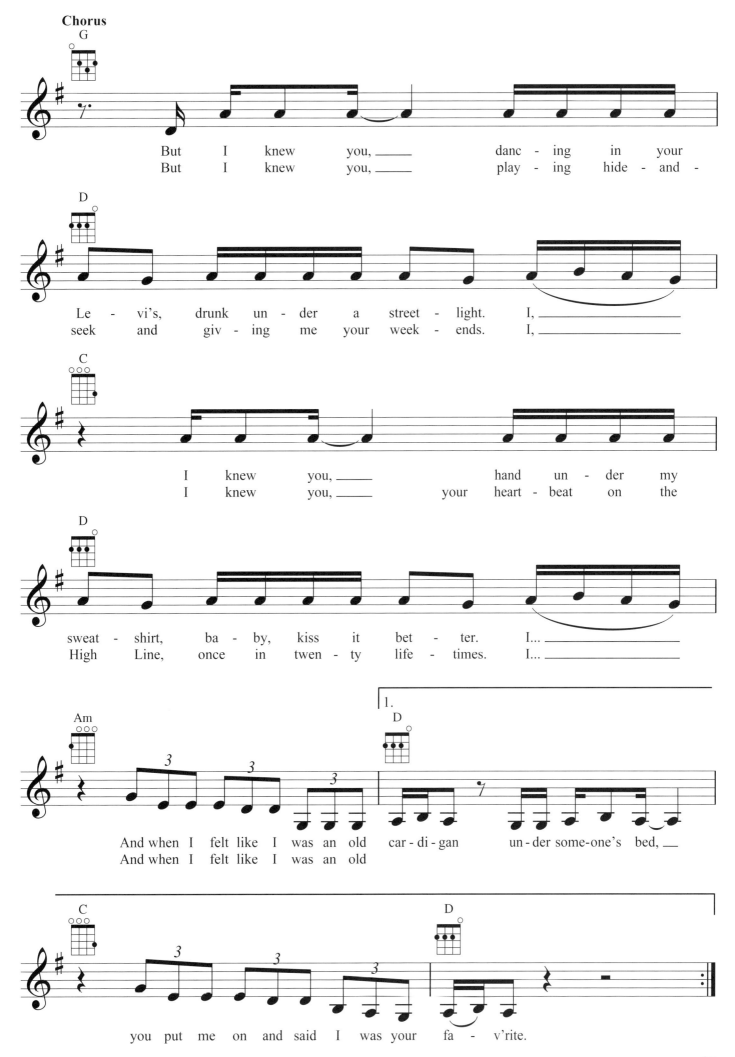

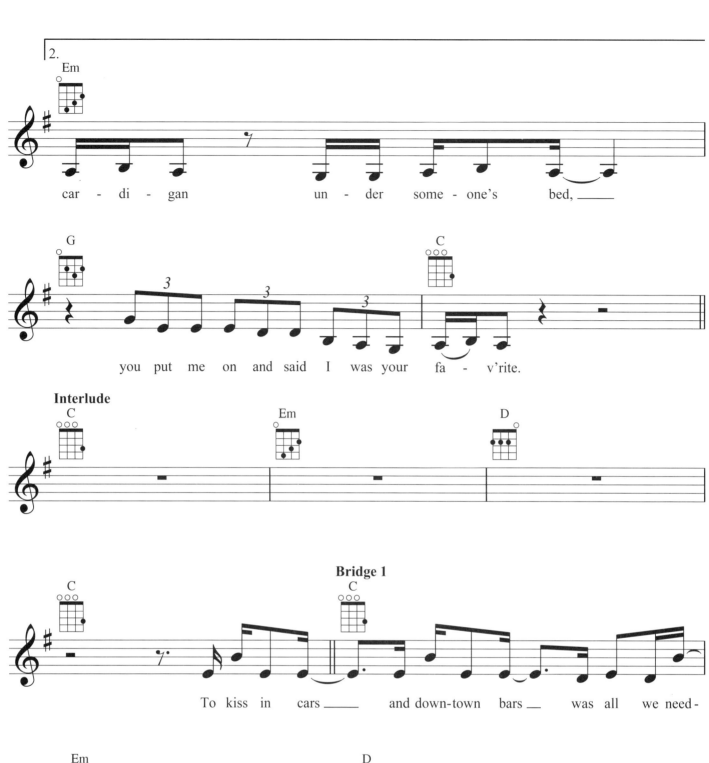

Interlude

Bridge 1

Chorus

last train, marked me like a blood - stain. I, _____

I knew you, _____ tried to change the

end - ing, Pe - ter los - ing Wen - dy. I, _____

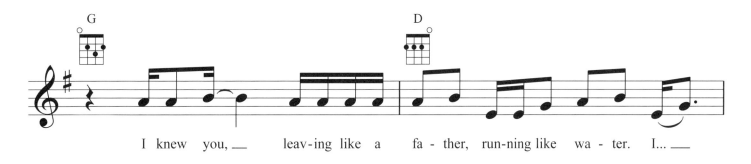

I knew you, _ leav-ing like a fa - ther, run-ning like wa - ter. I... _

And when you are young, they as - sume you know

Bridge 2

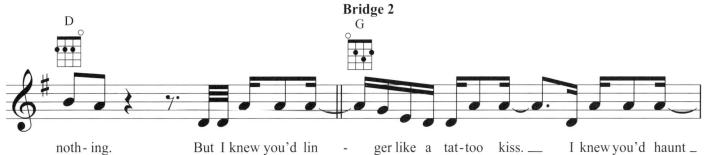

noth - ing. But I knew you'd lin - ger like a tat-too kiss. _ I knew you'd haunt _

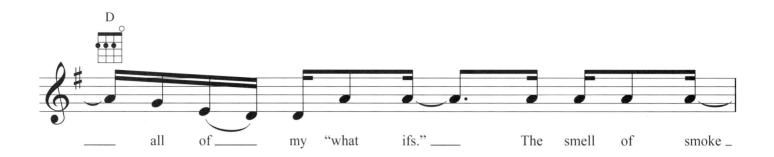

_____ all of _____ my "what ifs." _____ The smell of smoke _

_____ would hang a - round this long _____ 'cause I knew ev -

- 'ry - thing when I was young. _____ I knew I'd curse _

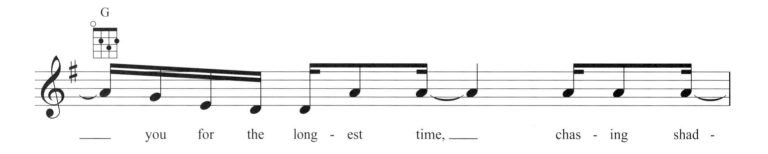

_____ you for the long - est time, _____ chas - ing shad -

- ows in the gro - c'ry line. _____ I knew you'd miss _

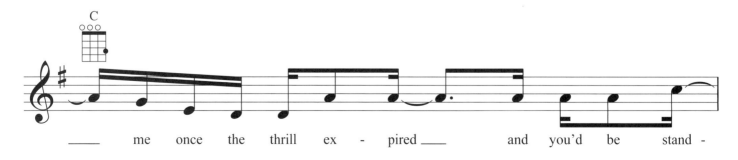

_____ me once the thrill ex - pired _____ and you'd be stand -

- ing in my front porch light. ___ And I knew you'd come back ___

___ to me, you'd come back ___ to me. And you'd come back ___

___ to me, and you'd come back. ___

Outro

And when I felt like I was an old

car - di - gan un - der some - one's bed, ___

you put me on and said I was your fa - v'rite.

Champagne Problems

Words and Music by Taylor Swift and William Bowery

First note

Verse
With motion

1. You booked the night train for a rea - son, so you could
2. You told your fam - 'ly for a rea - son; you

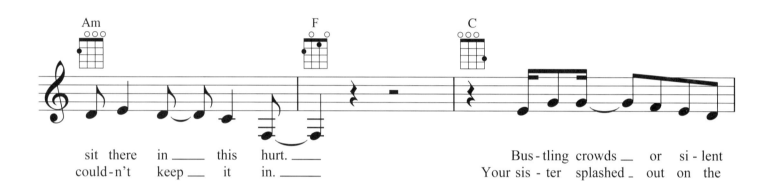

sit there in this hurt. Bus - tling crowds or si - lent
could-n't keep it in. Your sis - ter splashed out on the

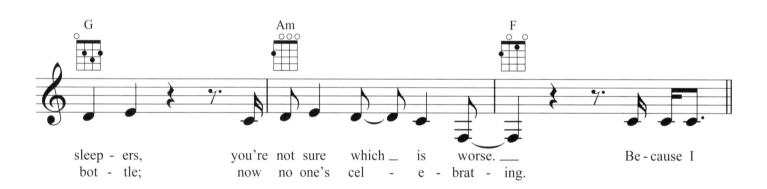

sleep - ers, you're not sure which is worse. Be - cause I
bot - tle; now no one's cel - e - brat - ing.

Chorus

dropped your hand while danc - ing, left you out there stand - ing
Dom Pé - ri - gnon, you brought it, no crowd of friends ap - plaud - ed.

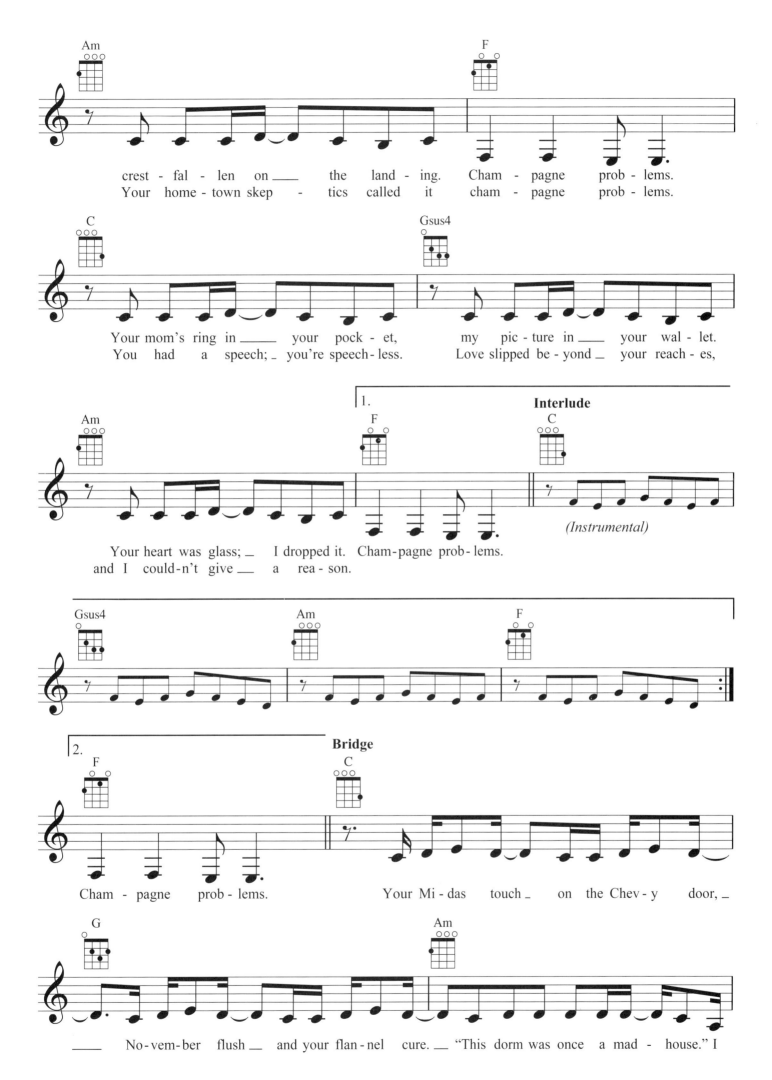

crest - fal - len on ____ the land - ing. Cham - pagne prob - lems.
Your home - town skep - tics called it cham - pagne prob - lems.

Your mom's ring in ____ your pock - et, my pic - ture in ____ your wal - let.
You had a speech; __ you're speech - less. Love slipped be - yond __ your reach - es,

1.

Interlude

Your heart was glass; __ I dropped it. Cham - pagne prob - lems.
and I could - n't give ____ a rea - son.

(Instrumental)

2.

Bridge

Cham - pagne prob - lems.

Your Mi - das touch _ on the Chev - y door, _

____ No - vem - ber flush _ and your flan - nel cure. __ "This dorm was once a mad - house." I

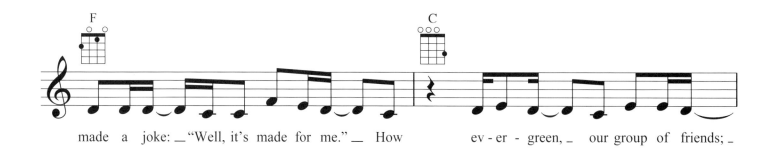

made a joke: __ "Well, it's made for me." __ How ev - er - green, __ our group of friends; __

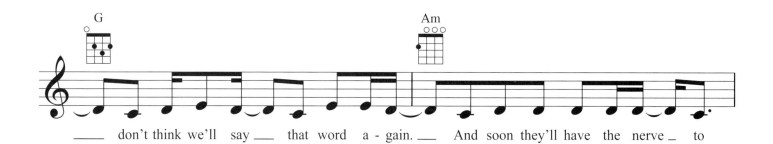

____ don't think we'll say ___ that word a - gain. ___ And soon they'll have the nerve _ to

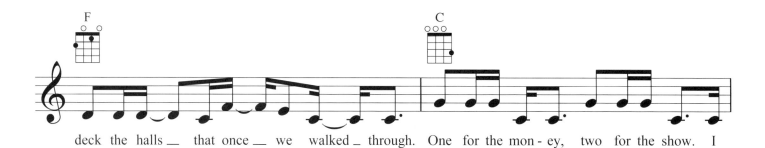

deck the halls __ that once __ we walked _ through. One for the mon - ey, two for the show. I

nev - er was read - y, so I watch you go. Some - times you just don't know the an - swer till

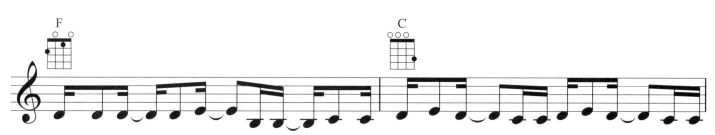

some - one's on ___ their knees _ and asks __ you. "She would've made _ such a love - ly bride. _ What a

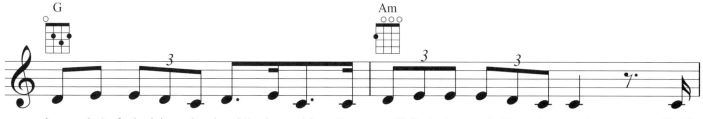

shame she's fucked in the head," they said. But you'll find the real thing in - stead. She'll

Delicate

Words and Music by Taylor Swift, Max Martin and Shellback

First note

Intro
Moderately

This ain't for the best.   My rep - u - ta - tion's nev - er been worse, so

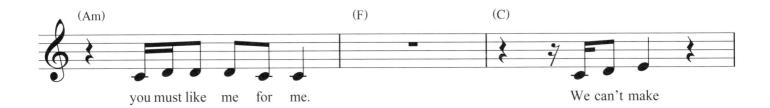

you must like me for me.   We can't make

an - y prom - i - ses, now can we, babe?   But you can make me a drink.

Verse

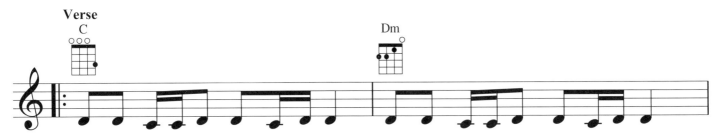

1. Dive bar on the East Side. Where you at?   Phone lights up my night - stand in the black.
2. Third floor on the West Side, me and you.   Hand-some, you're a man - sion with a view. Do the

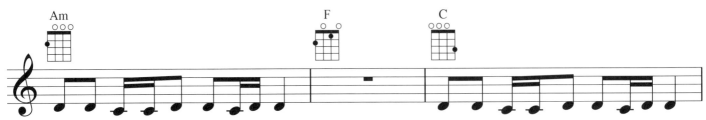

Come here, you can meet me in the back.   Dark jeans and your Ni - kes; look at you.
girls back home _ touch you like I do?   Long night with your hands up in my hair.

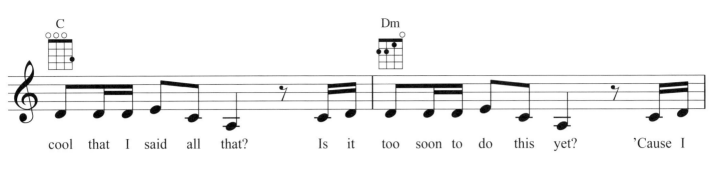

cool that I said all that?   Is it too soon to do this yet?   'Cause I

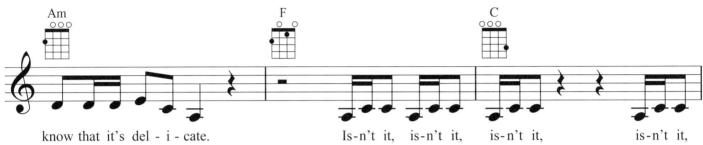

know that it's del - i - cate.   Is-n't it, is-n't it,   is-n't it,   is-n't it,

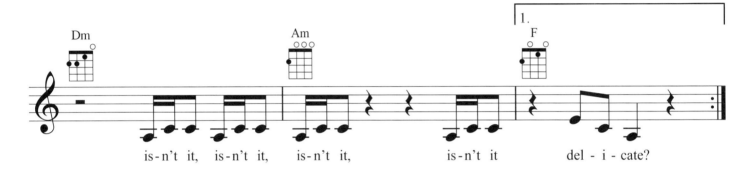

is-n't it, is-n't it,   is-n't it,   is-n't it   del - i - cate?

Bridge

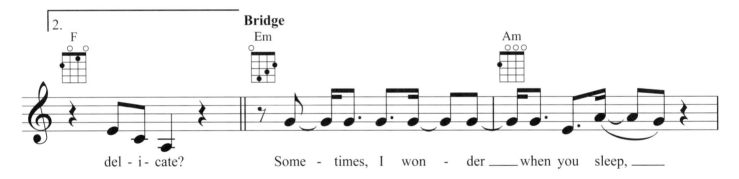

del - i - cate?   Some - times, I won - der ___ when you sleep, ___

are ___ you ev - er ___ dream - ing of me? _____

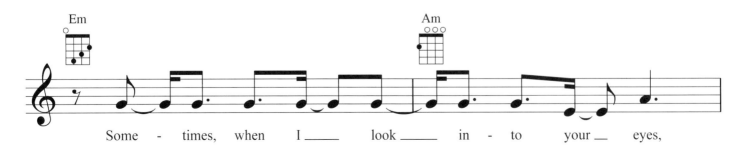

Some - times, when I ___ look ___ in - to your ___ eyes,

I ___ pre-tend you're _ mine   all ___ the damn time. _   Is it
                                                ('Cause I like ___

Chorus

cool that I said all that?   Is it chill that you're in my head?   'Cause I
___ you.)

know that it's del - i - cate.   (Del - i - cate.)   Is it
                                          (Yeah, I want _____

cool that I said all that?   Is it too soon to do this yet?   'Cause I
___ you.)

1.

know that it's del - i - cate.   (Del - i - cate.)   Is it
                                  ('Cause I want ___

2.

Del - i - cate.

Fearless

Words and Music by Taylor Swift, Liz Rose and Hillary Lindsey

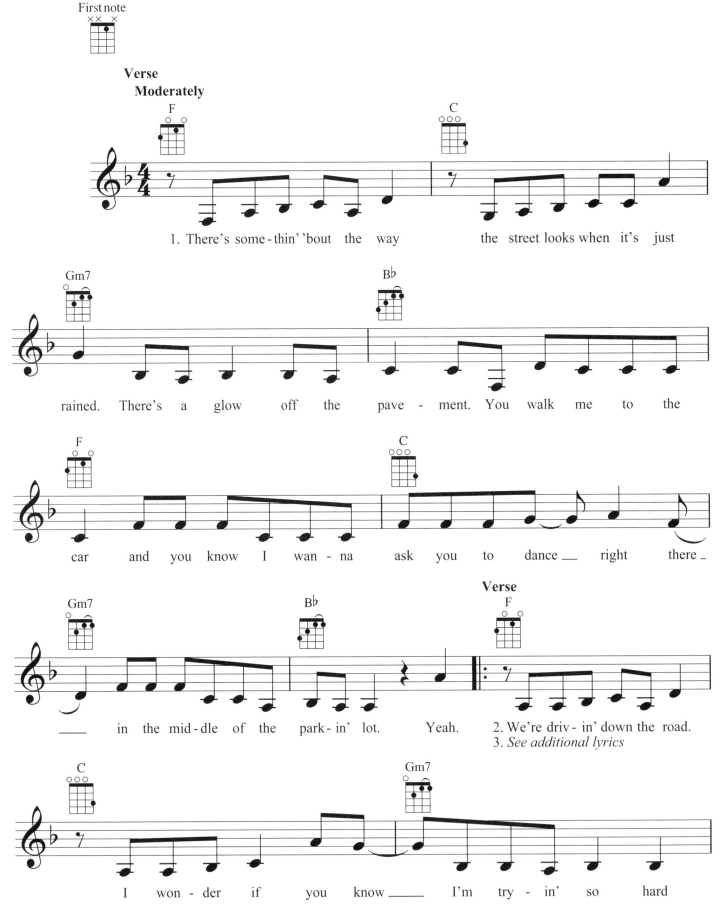

1. There's some-thin' 'bout the way the street looks when it's just rained. There's a glow off the pave-ment. You walk me to the car and you know I wan-na ask you to dance ___ right there ___ in the mid-dle of the park-in' lot. Yeah.

2. We're driv-in' down the road.

3. *See additional lyrics*

I won-der if you know ___ I'm try-in' so hard

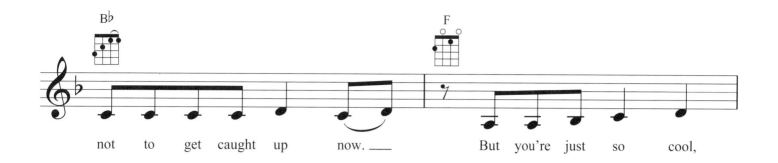

not to get caught up now. ___ But you're just so cool,

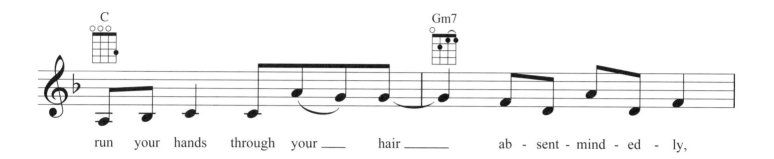

run your hands through your ___ hair ___ ab - sent - mind - ed - ly,

%. Chorus

mak - in' me want you. And I don't know how it gets bet - ter than

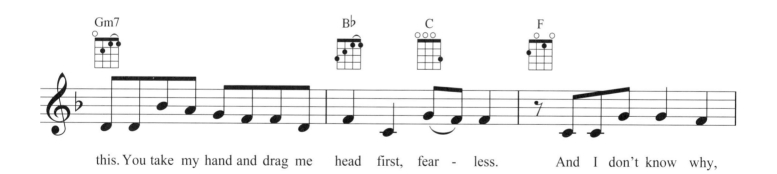

this. You take my hand and drag me head first, fear - less. And I don't know why,

To Coda ⊕

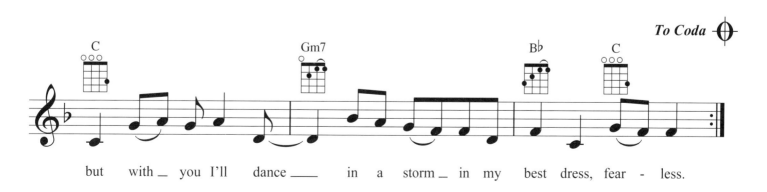

but with _ you I'll dance ___ in a storm _ in my best dress, fear - less.

Additional Lyrics

3. So, baby, drive slow
   Till we run out of road
   In this one-horse town.
   I wanna stay right here
   In this passenger seat.
   You put your hands on me
   In this moment.
   Now capture it, remember it.

Exile

Words and Music by Taylor Swift, William Bowery and Justin Vernon

First note

Verse
Moderately slow

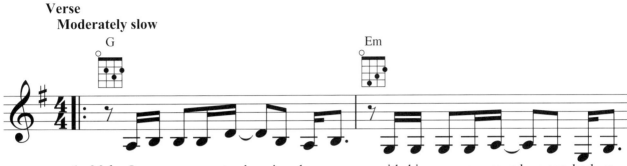

1. *Male:* I can see you stand - ing, hon - ey, with his arms a - round _ your bod - y.
2. *Female:* I can see you star - ing, hon - ey, like he's just your un - der - stud - y,

Laugh - ing, but the joke's _ not fun - ny at all.
like you'd get your knuck - les blood - y for me.

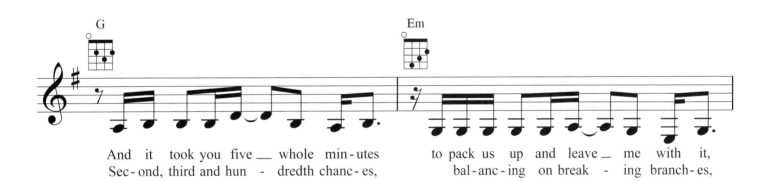

And it took you five _ whole min - utes to pack us up and leave _ me with it,
Sec - ond, third and hun - dredth chanc - es, bal - anc - ing on break - ing branch - es,

hold - ing all this love _ out here in the hall.
those _ eyes add in - sult to in - ju - ry.

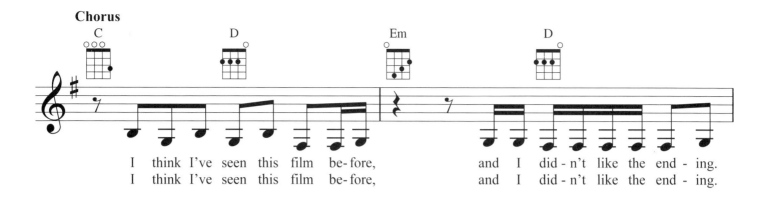

I think I've seen this film be-fore, and I did-n't like the end-ing.
I think I've seen this film be-fore, and I did-n't like the end-ing.

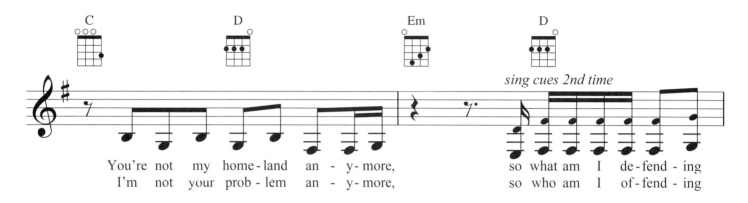

sing cues 2nd time

You're not my home-land an - y-more, so what am I de-fend-ing
I'm not your prob-lem an - y-more, so who am I of-fend-ing

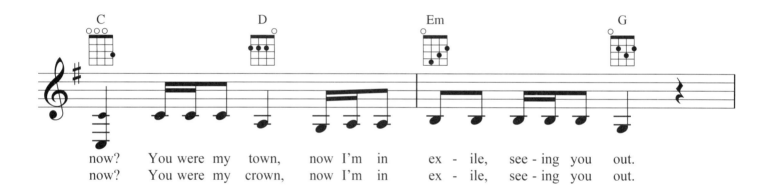

now? You were my town, now I'm in ex - ile, see-ing you out.
now? You were my crown, now I'm in ex - ile, see-ing you out.

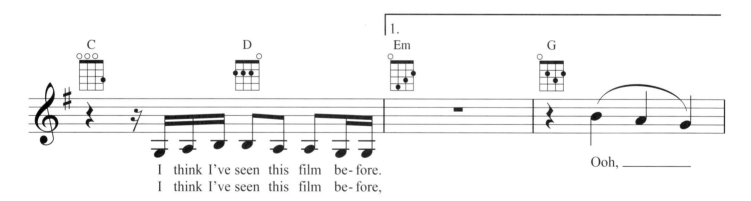

1.

I think I've seen this film be-fore.
I think I've seen this film be-fore,

Ooh, _____

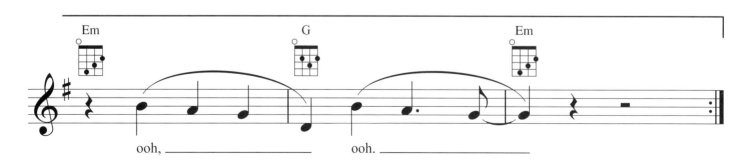

ooh, _____ ooh. _____

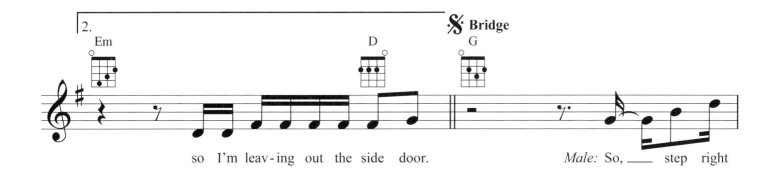

so I'm leav-ing out the side door. *Male:* So, ___ step right

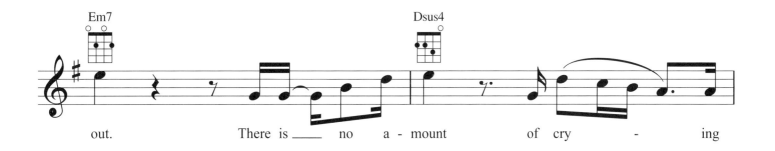

out. There is ___ no a - mount of cry - ing

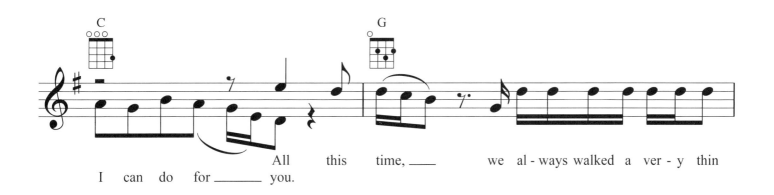

I can do for ___ you.

All this time, ___ we al - ways walked a ver - y thin

line. You did-n't e -ven hear me out. You nev - er gave a warn - ing

Female: Did-n't e - ven hear me out. I

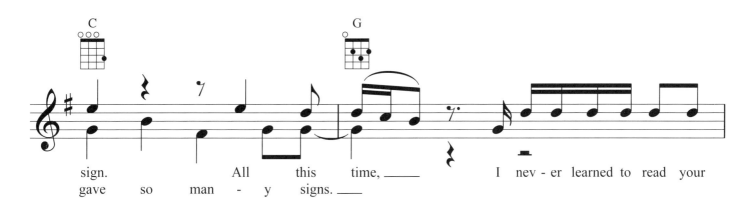

sign. All this time, ___ I nev - er learned to read your

gave so man - y signs. ___

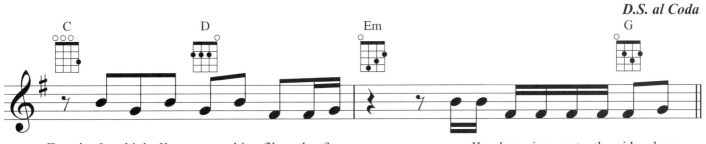

Female: I think I've seen this film be-fore, so I'm leav-ing out the side door.

Coda

sign. All this time, ___ I nev-er learned to read your

gave so man - y signs, ___ so man - y times, _

mind, I could-n't turn things a - round. You nev-er gave a warn-ing

___ so man - y signs. ___ *Male:* You

sign, nev-er gave a warn-ing sign.

nev-er gave a warn-ing sign.

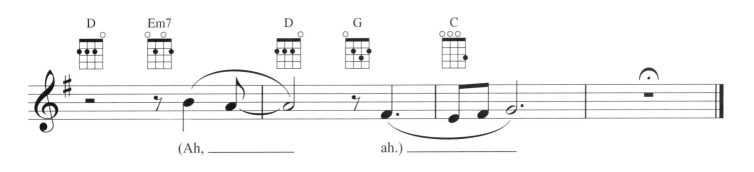

(Ah, ___ ah.) ___

I Knew You Were Trouble

Words and Music by Taylor Swift, Shellback and Max Martin

Bridge

sad - dest fear   comes   creep - ing   in,

that you   nev - er   loved   me   or   her, _____   or

D.S. al Coda

an - y - one   or   an - y - thing.   Yeah, _____

Coda   **Outro**

trou - ble,   trou - ble.   I   knew   you   were   trou - ble when   you   walked   in. _____

_____ Trou - ble,   trou - ble,   trou - ble.   I   knew   you   were

trou - ble when   you   walked   in. _____   Trou - ble,   trou - ble,   trou - ble.

Look What You Made Me Do

**Words and Music by Taylor Swift, Jack Antonoff,
Richard Fairbrass, Fred Fairbrass and Rob Manzoli**

First note

Verse
Urban Pop

N.C. (Am)

1. I don't like your lit - tle games, don't
2. I don't like your per - fect crime, how

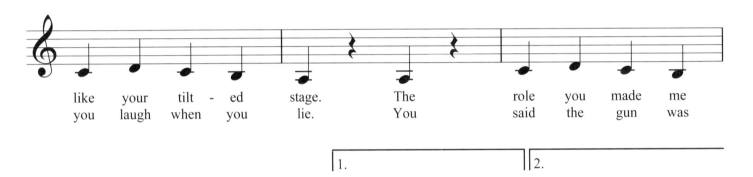

like your tilt - ed stage. The role you made me
you laugh when you lie. You said the gun was

1.

2.

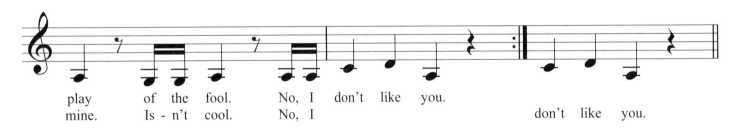

play of the fool. No, I don't like you.
mine. Is - n't cool. No, I don't like you.

Pre-Chorus

Am   Am7

But I got smart - er, I got hard - er in the nick of time.   Hon - ey, I rose up from the

dead, I do it all the time. I've got a list of names and yours is in red, un-der-lined.

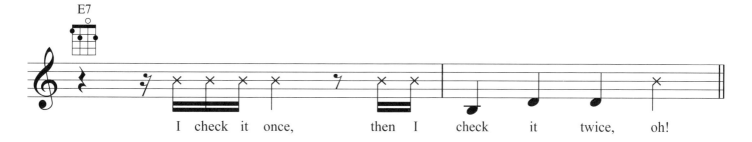

I check it once, then I check it twice, oh!

Chorus

N.C. (Am)

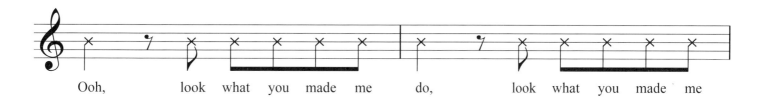

Ooh, look what you made me do, look what you made me

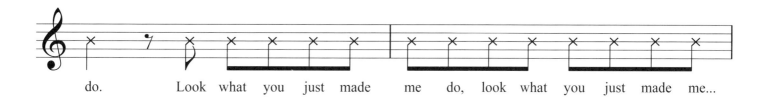

do. Look what you just made me do, look what you just made me...

To Coda

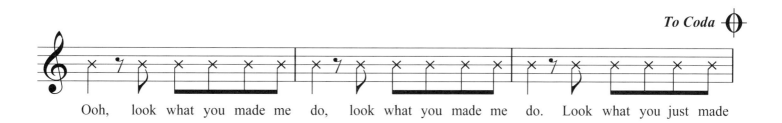

Ooh, look what you made me do, look what you made me do. Look what you just made

Verse

N.C. (Am)

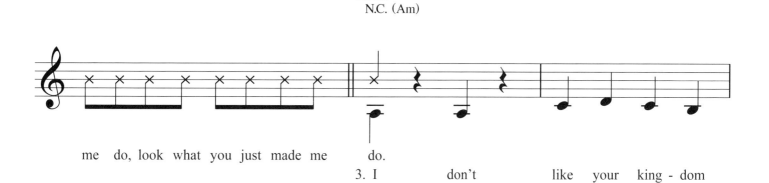

me do, look what you just made me do.

3. I don't like your king-dom

keys,   they   once be - longed to   me.   You

asked me for a place to sleep,   locked me out   and threw a feast.

Pre-Chorus

N.C. (Am)

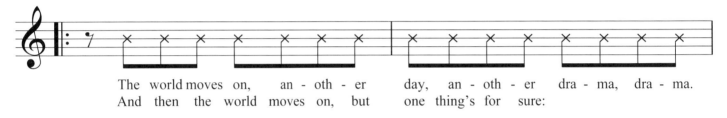

The world moves on,   an - oth - er   day, an - oth - er   dra - ma, dra - ma.
And then the world moves on, but   one thing's for   sure:

1.

But not   for   me, not for me,   all   I   think a - bout is kar - ma.
May - be   I   got mine, but you'll

2.

D.S. al Coda

$\oplus$ **Coda**

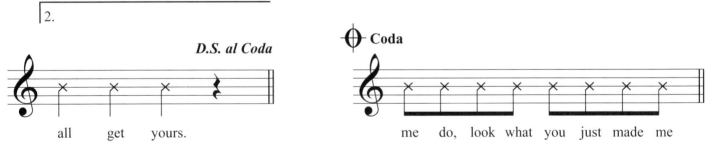

all   get   yours.   me   do, look what you just made me

Bridge

Am   F

do.
I don't trust no - bod - y and no - bod - y trusts me.   I'll be the ac - tress

(Spoken:) *"I'm sorry, the old Taylor can't come to the phone right now.*

Why?   Oh,   'cause she's dead!"

Outro-Chorus

N.C. (Am)

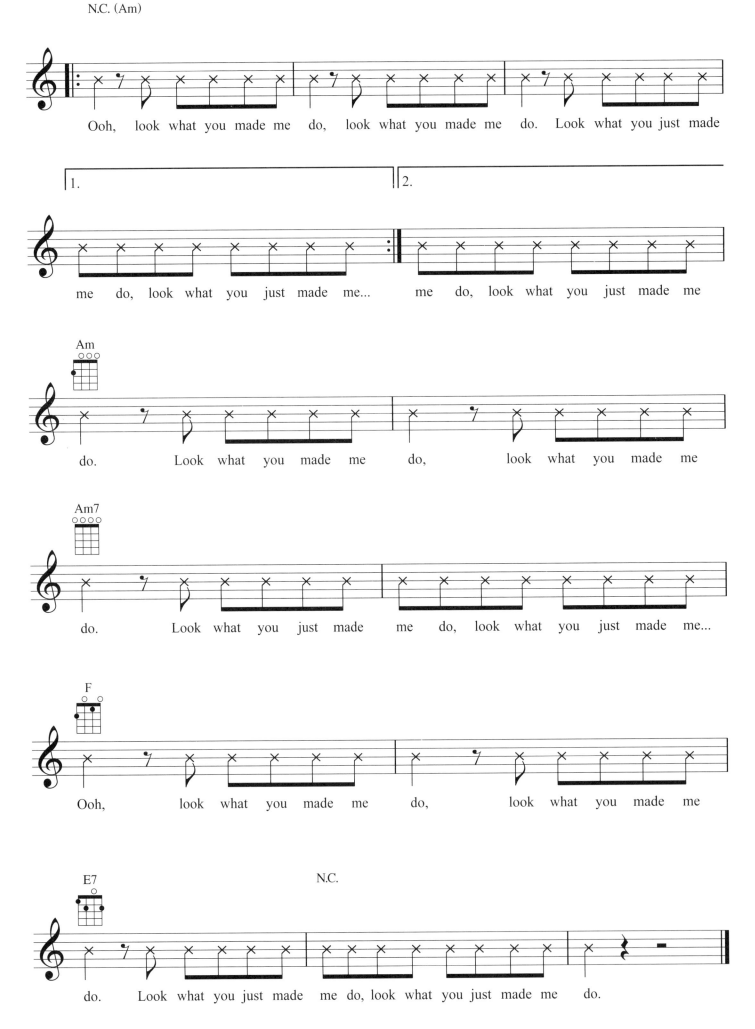

Ooh, look what you made me do, look what you made me do. Look what you just made

1.
me do, look what you just made me...

2.
me do, look what you just made me

Am
do. Look what you made me do, look what you made me

Am7
do. Look what you just made me do, look what you just made me...

F
Ooh, look what you made me do, look what you made me

E7
do. Look what you just made me do, look what you just made me

N.C.
do.

46

Love Story

Words and Music by Taylor Swift

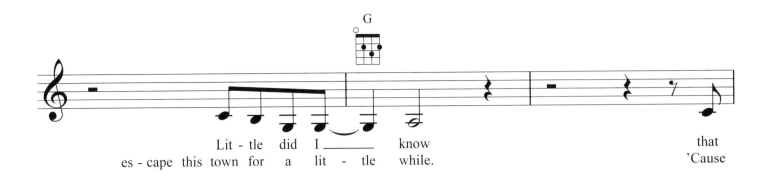

G

Lit - tle did I _____ know   that
es - cape this town for a lit - tle while.   'Cause

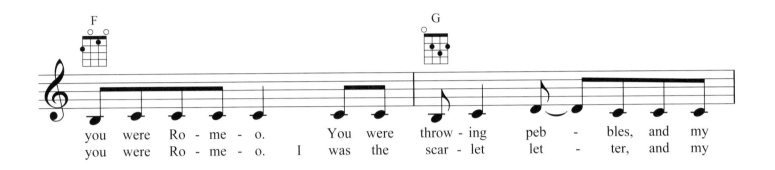

F   G

you were Ro - me - o.   You were throw - ing peb - bles, and my
you were Ro - me - o. I was the scar - let let - ter, and my

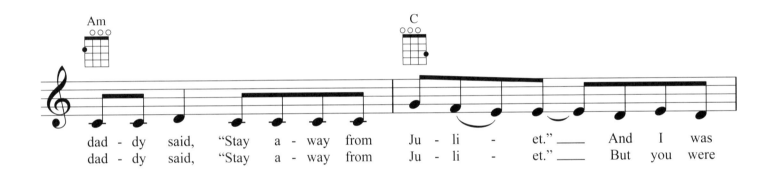

Am   C

dad - dy said, "Stay a - way from Ju - li - et." ____ And I was
dad - dy said, "Stay a - way from Ju - li - et." ____ But you were

F   G   Am

cry - in' on the stair - case,   beg - gin' you, "Please __ don't go." ____
ev - 'ry - thing to me. I was

𝄋 **Chorus**

F   G   C

And I _____ said,   "Ro - me - o, take me some - where we can be a - lone.
(D.S.) "Ro - me - o, save me. I've been feel - ing so a - lone.

I'll be wait - ing. All there's left to do is run. You'll be the prince and
I keep wait - ing for you, but you nev - er come. Is this in my head? I don't

To Coda ✛

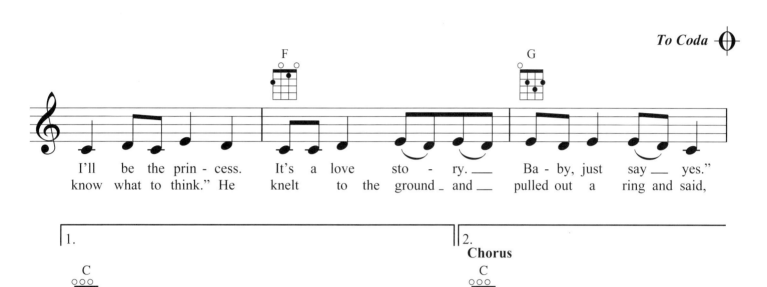

I'll be the prin - cess. It's a love sto - ry. __ Ba - by, just say __ yes."
know what to think." He knelt to the ground _ and __ pulled out a ring and said,

1.

2. **Chorus**

3. So, "Ro - me - o, save me. They're

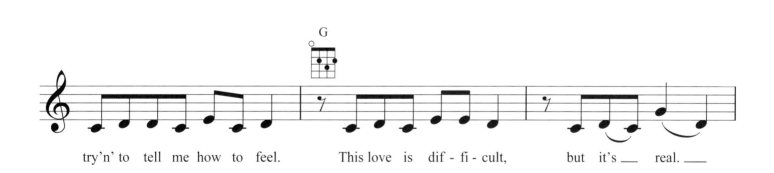

try'n' to tell me how to feel. This love is dif - fi - cult, but it's __ real. __

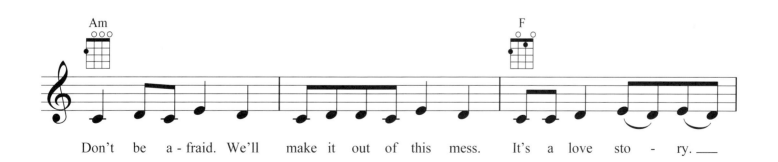

Don't be a - fraid. We'll make it out of this mess. It's a love sto - ry. __

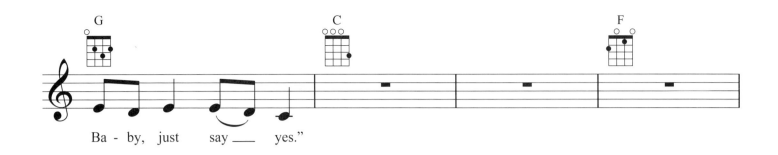

Ba - by, just say ___ yes."

Bridge

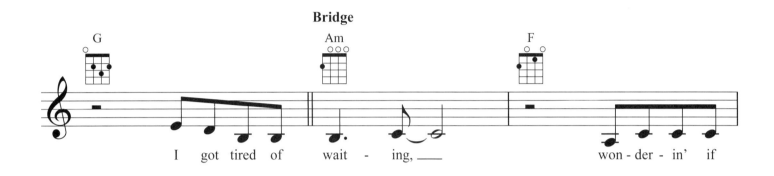

I got tired of wait - ing, ___ won - der - in' if

you were ev - er com - ing a - round. ___ My faith in you was fad - ing ___

D.S. al Coda

___ when I met you on the out - skirts of town. And I said,

Chorus

Coda

"Mar - ry me, Ju - li - et, you nev - er have to be a - lone.

I love you __ and that's all I real-ly know. I talked to your dad. Go

pick out a white dress. It's a love sto - ry. __ Ba - by, just say __

Outro

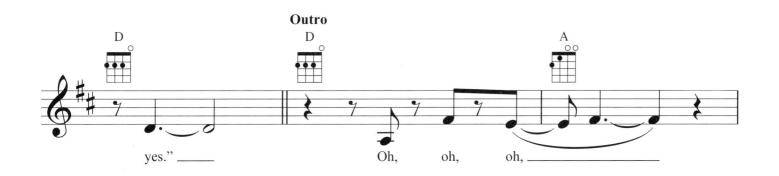

yes." _____ Oh, oh, oh, _____

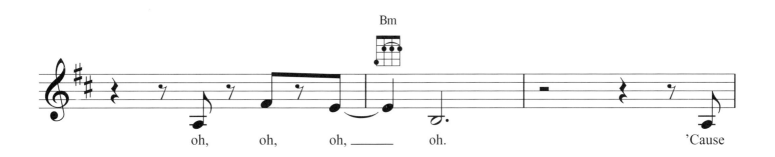

oh, oh, oh, _____ oh. 'Cause

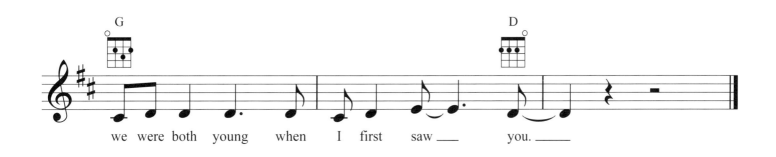

we were both young when I first saw __ you. __

ME!

Words and Music by Taylor Swift, Joel Little and Brendon Urie

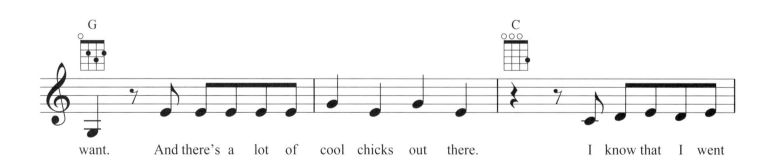

psy - cho on the phone. I nev - er leave ___ well e - nough a -

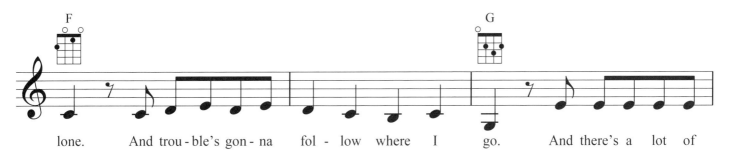

lone. And trou - ble's gon - na fol - low where I go. And there's a lot of

Pre-Chorus

N.C.

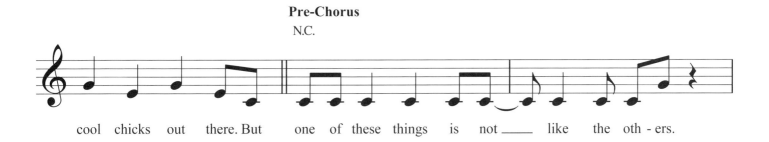

cool chicks out there. But one of these things is not ___ like the oth - ers.

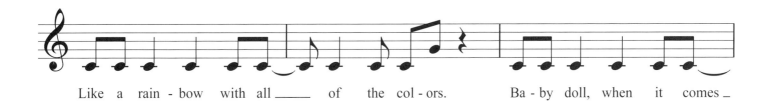

Like a rain - bow with all ___ of the col - ors. Ba - by doll, when it comes ___

___ to a lov - er, I prom - ise that you'll nev - er find an - oth - er like me, ee

Chorus

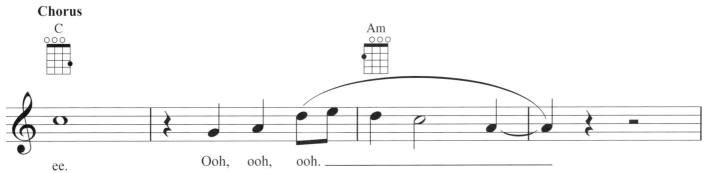

ee. Ooh, ooh, ooh. ___

I'm the on - ly one of me. _____ Ba - by, that's the fun of me,

ee ee ee. _____ Ooh, ooh, ooh. _____

_____ You're the on - ly one of you. _____

Ba - by, that's the fun of you. _____ And I prom - ise that no - bod - y's gon - na

Verse

love you like me, ee ee. *Male:* 2. I know I tend to make it a - bout

me. I know you nev - er get just what you see. But I will nev - er

54

bore you, ba - by. And there's a lot of lame guys out there.

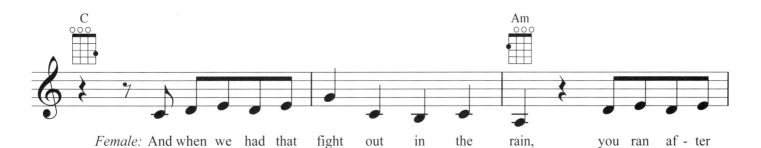

Female: And when we had that fight out in the rain, you ran af - ter

me and called my name. *Male:* I nev - er wan - na see you walk a -

Pre-Chorus

N.C.

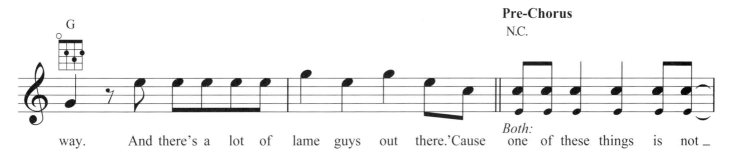

way. And there's a lot of lame guys out there. 'Cause one of these things is not _

Both:

_ like the oth - ers. Liv - ing in win - ter, I _____ am your sum - mer.

Ba - by doll, when it comes _ to a lov - er, *Male:* I prom - ise that you'll nev - er find an -

55

oth - er like me, ee ee. Ooh, ooh, ooh. _____

_____ *Male:* I'm the on - ly one of me. _____

{ Let me keep you com-pa - ny, }
{ Ba - by, that's the fun of me, } ee ee ee. _____ Ooh, ooh, ooh. __

_____ *Male:* You're the on - ly one of you. __

__ Ba - by, that's the fun of you. _____ *Both:* And I

prom - ise that no - bod - y's gon - na love you like me, ee ee. Hey, kids,

56

Bridge

spell - ing   is   fun!   Girl,   there   ain't   no   I _____ in   team,

but   you   know   there   is _____   a   me.   Strike   the   band   up,   one, _

_____   two,   three.   *Female:* I   prom-ise   that you'll nev - er   find   an - oth - er   like   me.

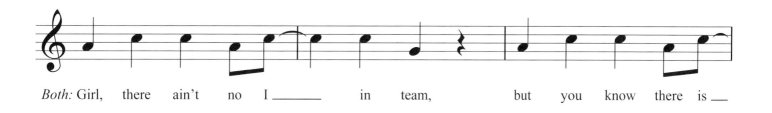

Both: Girl,   there   ain't   no   I _____   in   team,   but   you   know   there   is _

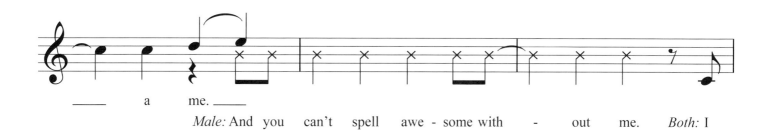

_____   a   me. _____

    Male: And   you   can't   spell   awe - some   with   -   out   me.   *Both:* I

D.S. al Coda

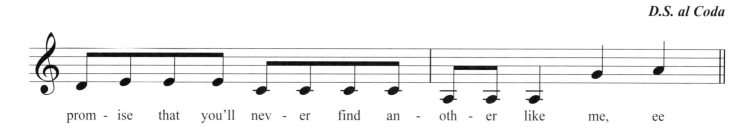

prom - ise   that   you'll   nev - er   find   an - oth - er   like   me,   ee

Outro-Chorus

ee.
Girl, there ain't no I _____ in team, but you know there is _____ a me. _____

I'm the on - ly one of me. _____ Ba - by, that's the fun of me,

ee ee ee. Strike the band up, one, _____ two, three. You

can't spell awe - some with - out me. _____ You're the on - ly one of you. _____

_____ Ba - by, that's the fun of you. _____ And I

prom - ise that no - bod - y's gon - na love you like me, ee ee.

Lover

Words and Music by Taylor Swift

First note

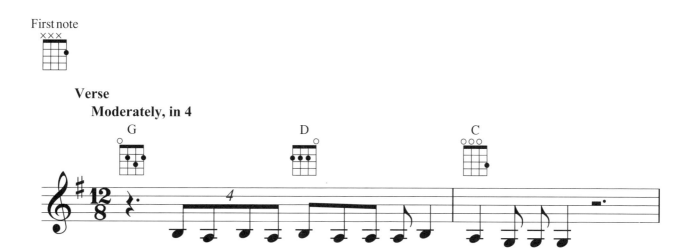

Verse
Moderately, in 4

1. We could leave the Christ-mas lights up 'til Jan - u - ar - y.

This is our place; we make the rules. ___ And there's a

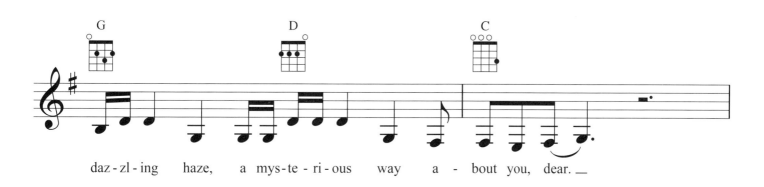

daz - zl - ing haze, a mys - te - ri - ous way a - bout you, dear. ___

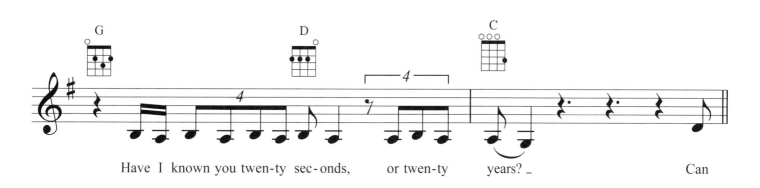

Have I known you twen-ty sec-onds, or twen-ty years? ___ Can

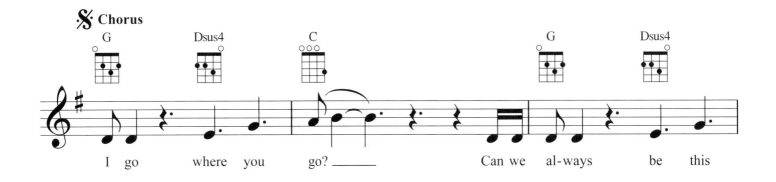

Chorus

I go where you go? _____ Can we al-ways be this

close? _____ For - ev - er and ev - er, ah, _____ take me out and take me

home. _ You're my, _____ my, _____ my, _____ my _____

To Coda

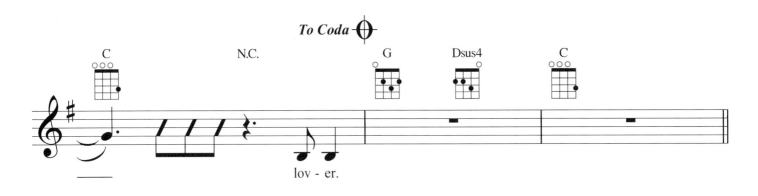

_____ lov - er.

Verse

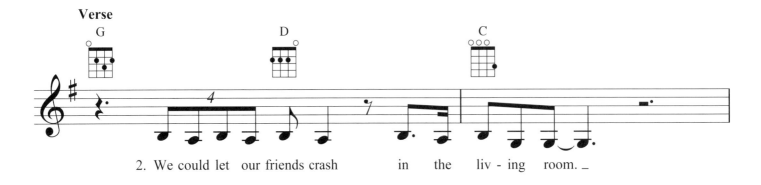

2. We could let our friends crash in the liv - ing room. _

This is our place; we make the call. ___ I'm

high-ly sus-pi-cious that ev-'ry-one who sees you wants ___ you. ___ I've

D.S. al Coda

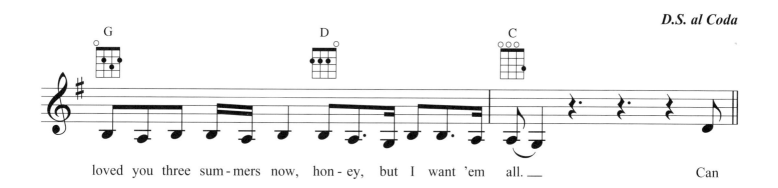

loved you three sum-mers now, hon-ey, but I want 'em all. ___ Can

Coda
Bridge

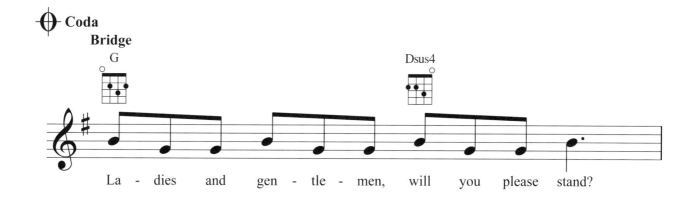

La - dies and gen - tle - men, will you please stand?

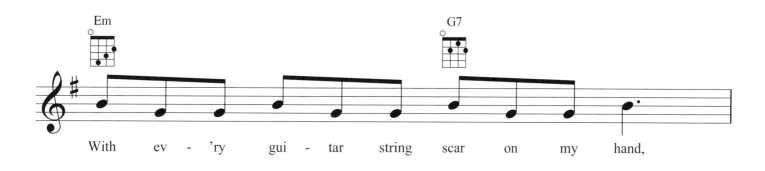

With ev - 'ry gui - tar string scar on my hand,

I take this mag - net - ic force of a man to be my lov - er. ____

My heart's been bor - rowed and yours has been blue.

All's well that ends well, to end up with you.

Swear to be o - ver - dra - mat - ic and true __ to my lov - er. ____ And

you'll save all your dirt - i - est jokes for me. And at ev - 'ry

ta - ble __ I'll save you a seat, lov - er. ____ Can

Outro-Chorus

Mean

Words and Music by Taylor Swift

big e-nough so you can't hit me, and all you're

ev-er gon-na be is mean.

Why you got-ta be so ___

To Coda

___ mean?

Verse

2. You, with your switch-ing sides and your wild-fire lies and your

hu-mil-i-a-tion. You have point-ed out ___ my flaws ___

___ a-gain, __ as if I don't al-read-y see them. I walk with my ___

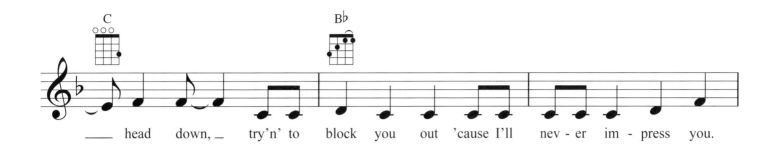

head down, __ try'n' to block you out 'cause I'll nev-er im-press you.

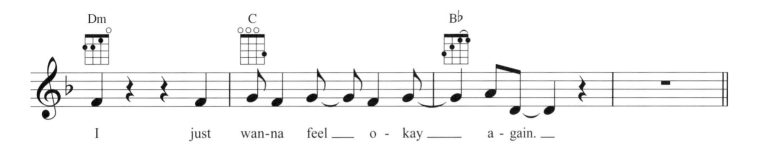

I just wan-na feel __ o-kay __ a - gain. __

Pre-Chorus

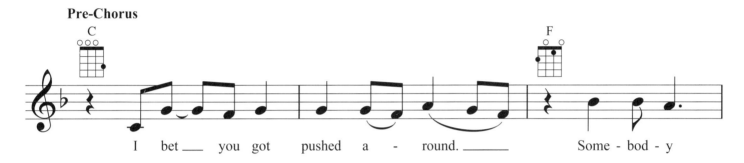

I bet __ you got pushed a - round. _____ Some-bod-y

made you __ cold. But the cy-cle ends __ right now __ 'cause you _

__ can't lead __ me down __ that road, __ and you __ don't know __ what you _

⊕ Coda   **Bridge**

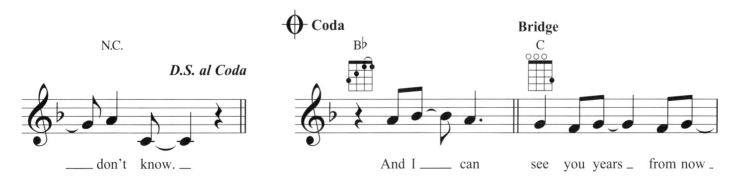

D.S. al Coda

__ don't know. __   And I __ can see you years _ from now _

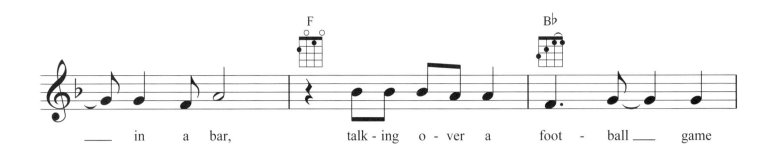

_____ in a bar, talk - ing o - ver a foot - ball _____ game

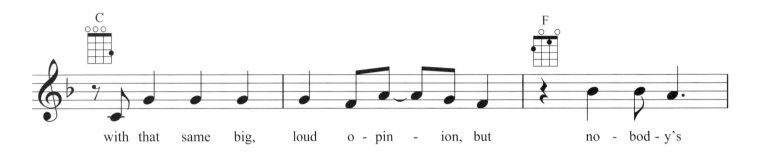

with that same big, loud o - pin - ion, but no - bod - y's

lis - ten - ing. Washed up and rant - ing a - bout the same old

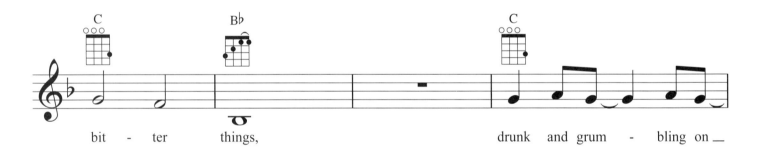

bit - ter things, drunk and grum - bling on _____

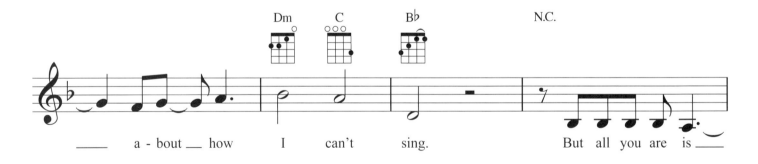

_____ a - bout _____ how I can't sing. But all you are is _____

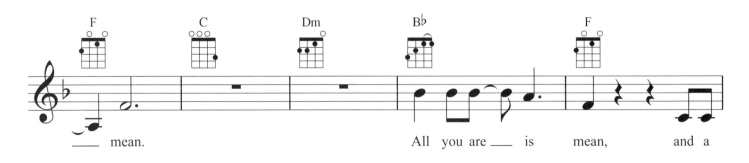

_____ mean. All you are _____ is mean, and a

Outro-Chorus

li - ar,   and pa - thet-ic,   and a - lone in life, __ and   mean   and

mean   and   mean   and   mean.   But   some - day __ }
                                          Some - day __ }

I'll   be __   liv-ing in a big ole   cit - y,   and   all   you're _

ev - er gon-na be   is   mean.   Yeah, __   some - day __   I'll   be __

big e-nough so you can't   hit   me,   and   all   you're   ev - er gon-na be   is

1.   2.

mean.   Why you got - ta   be   so...   Why you got - ta be   so _____ mean?

Mine

Words and Music by Taylor Swift

as we're ly-ing on the couch,
we got noth-in' fig-ured out.
the mo - ment I could see __ it.
When it was hard to take,

Yes, __ yes, __ I can see it now.
yes, __ yes, __ this __ is what I thought a - bout:

Chorus

Do you re-mem-ber? We were sit - tin' there by the wa - ter.

You put your arm a - round me __ for the first time.

You made a reb - el of a care - less man's care - ful daugh - ter.

1.

You are the best thing that's ev - er been mine. __

care-less man's care-ful daugh-ter. She is the best _ thing that's ev - er been _ mine." _

Outro

(Hold _ on _ and make it last. Hold _ on, _ nev - er turn back.)

You made a reb - el of a care - less's man's care - ful daugh - ter.

You are the best thing that's ev - er been mine. _____

(Hold __ on.) __

___ Do you be - lieve _ it? (Hold _ on.) __ We're gon - na make it now.

(Hold _ on.) __ And I can see _ it.

No Body, No Crime

Words and Music by Taylor Swift

First note

Verse
Moderately, in 2

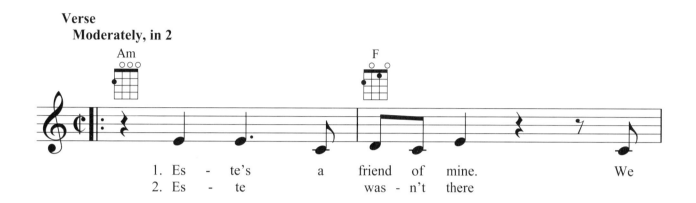

1. Es - te's   a   friend   of   mine.   We
2. Es - te   was - n't   there

meet up ev - 'ry Tues - day night for   din - ner   and   a   glass ___ of ___
Tues - day night at Ol - ive Gar - den,   at   her   job   or   an - y -

wine. Es - te's   been   los - in' sleep.   Her   hus - band's act - in' dif - f'rent and it
where. He re - ports his miss - in' wife,   and I   no - ticed when I passed his house his

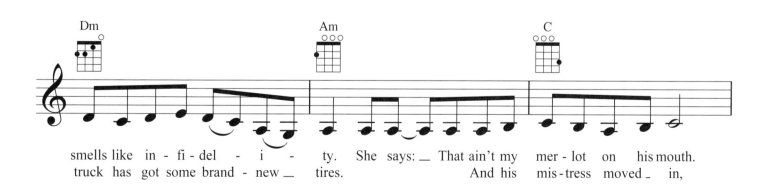

smells like in - fi - del - i - ty.   She says: ___ That ain't my mer - lot on his mouth.
truck has got some brand - new ___ tires.   And his mis - tress moved ___ in,

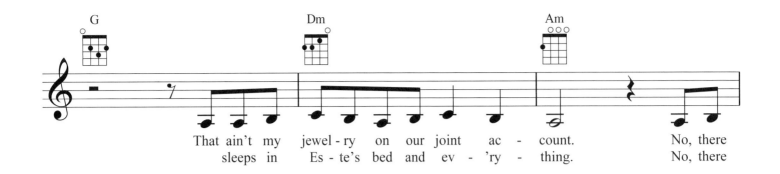

That ain't my jewel - ry on our joint ac - count. No, there
sleeps in Es - te's bed and ev - 'ry - thing. No, there

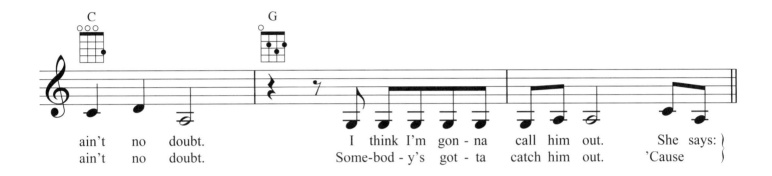

ain't no doubt. I think I'm gon - na call him out. She says:
ain't no doubt. Some - bod - y's got - ta catch him out. 'Cause

Chorus

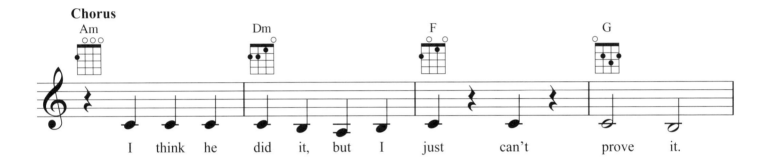

I think he did it, but I just can't prove it.

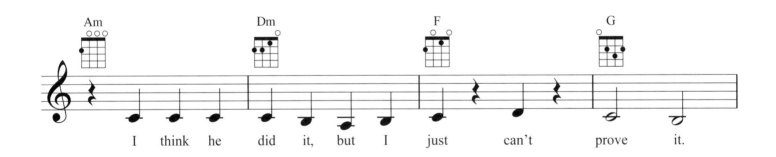

I think he did it, but I just can't prove it.

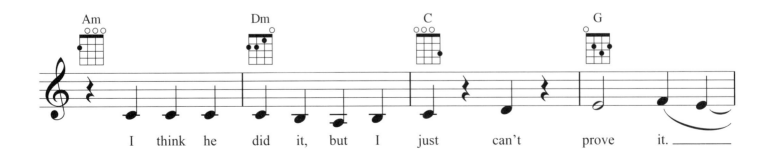

I think he did it, but I just can't prove it. _____

No, no bod - y, no crime. But I ain't let - tin' up un - til the

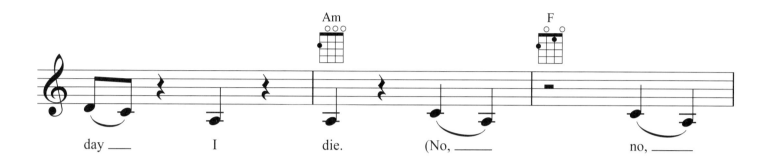

day ____ I die. (No, ____ no, ____

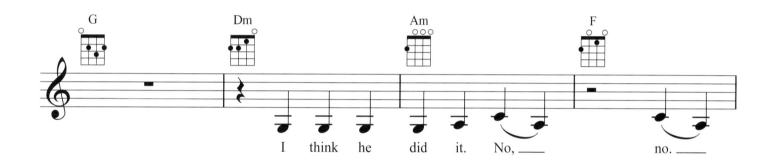

I think he did it. No, ____ no. ____

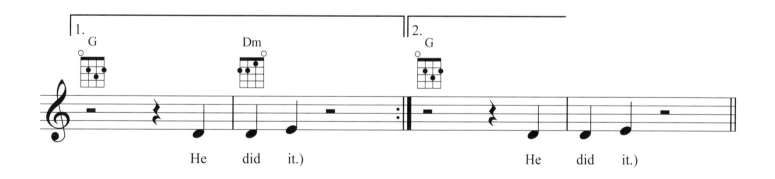

1.
He did it.)
2.
He did it.)

Bridge

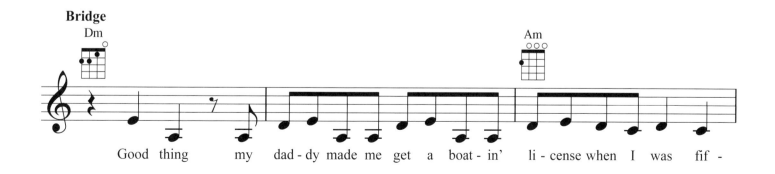

Good thing my dad - dy made me get a boat - in' li - cense when I was fif -

teen. _____ And I've cleaned e - nough __ hous - es to know how _

_____ to cov - er up a scene. _____ Good thing Es - te's

sis-ter's gon - na swear _____ she was with me. _____ Good thing his

Chorus

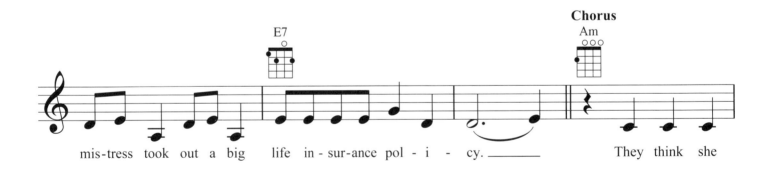

mis-tress took out a big life in - sur-ance pol - i - cy. _____ They think she

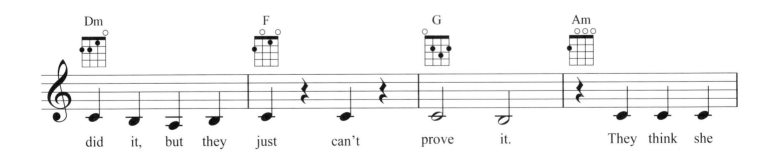

did it, but they just can't prove it. They think she

The 1

Words and Music by Taylor Swift and Aaron Dessner

Pre-Chorus

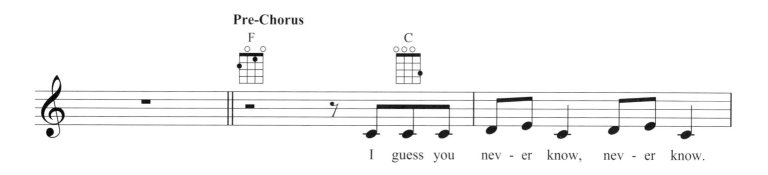

I guess you nev - er know, nev - er know.

And if you want - ed me, you real - ly should-'ve showed. And if you

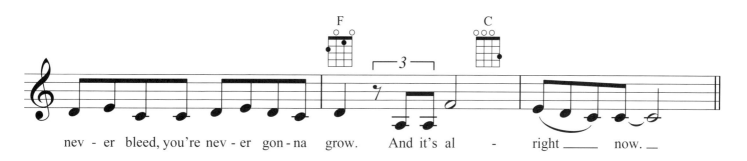

nev - er bleed, you're nev - er gon - na grow. And it's al - right ___ now. __

Chorus

But we were some - thing; don't you think so? Roar - ing

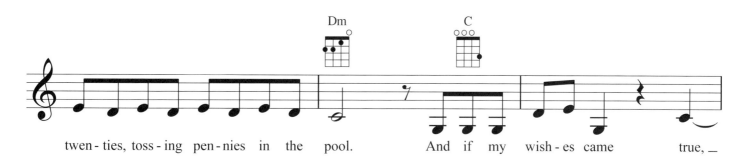

twen - ties, toss - ing pen - nies in the pool. And if my wish - es came true, __

___ it would-'ve been you. ___ In

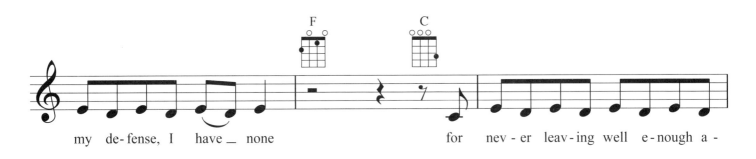

my de-fense, I have _ none   for nev-er leav-ing well e-nough a-

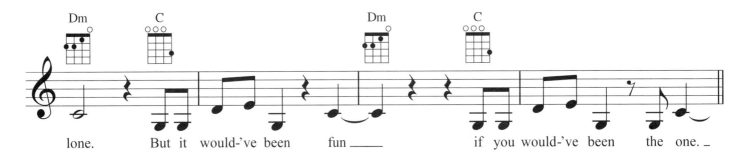

lone.   But it would've been   fun _____   if you would've been   the one. _

Interlude

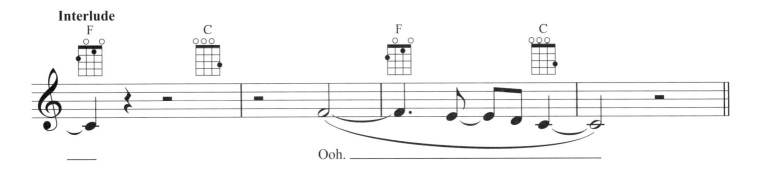

_   Ooh. _____

Verse

2. I had this dream: you're do-ing cool shit,   hav-ing ad-

ven-tures on your own.   You meet some wom-an on the in-ter-net and

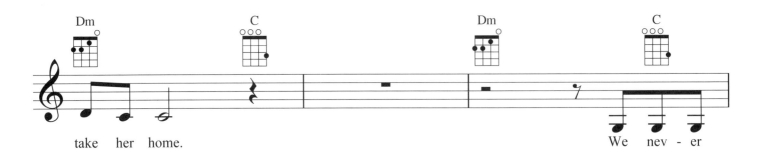

take her home.   We nev-er

paint - ed by the num - bers, ba - by, but we were mak - ing it count.

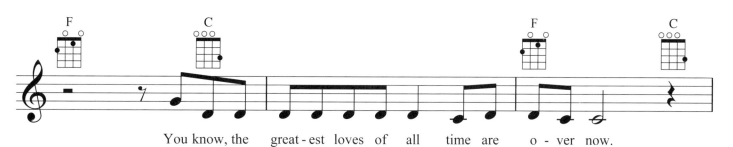

You know, the great - est loves of all time are o - ver now.

Pre-Chorus

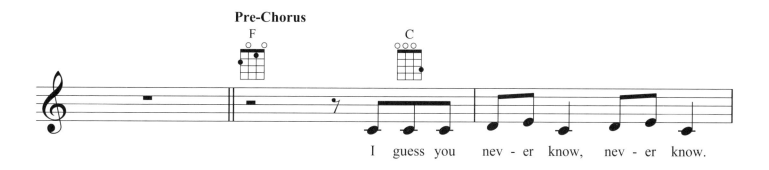

I guess you nev - er know, nev - er know.

Chorus

And it's an - oth - er day wak - ing up a - lone. ___ But we were

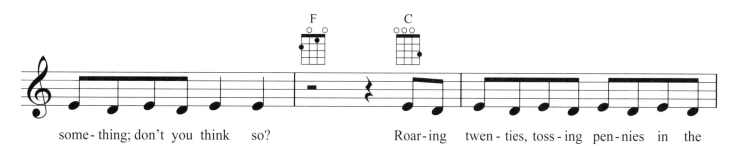

some - thing; don't you think so? Roar - ing twen - ties, toss - ing pen - nies in the

pool. And if my wish - es came true, ___ it

Chorus

We were some-thing; don't you think so? Ro - sé

flow-ing with your cho-sen fam - i - ly. And it would've been sweet __

____ if it could-'ve been me. _____ In

my de-fense, I have __ none for dig-ging up the grave an - oth - er

time. But it would-'ve been fun ____ if you would-'ve been the one.

Outro

Ooh. _____

Shake It Off

Words and Music by Taylor Swift, Max Martin and Shellback

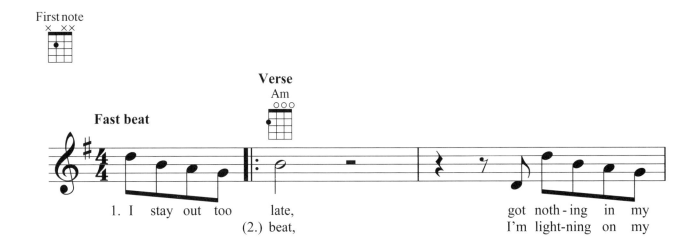

First note

Verse

Fast beat

1. I stay out too late,   got noth-ing in my
(2.) beat,   I'm light-ning on my

brain.   That's what peo-ple say, _____ mm,
feet.   And that's what they don't see, _____ mm,

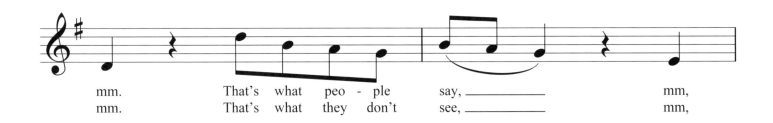

mm.   That's what peo-ple say, _____ mm,
mm.   That's what they don't see, _____ mm,

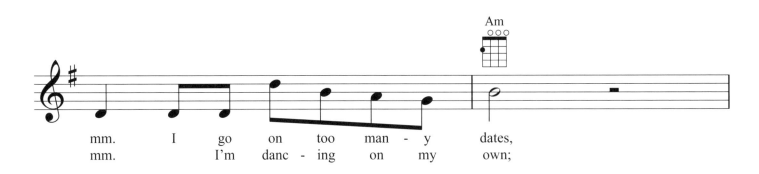

mm.   I go on too man - y dates,
mm.   I'm danc-ing on my own;

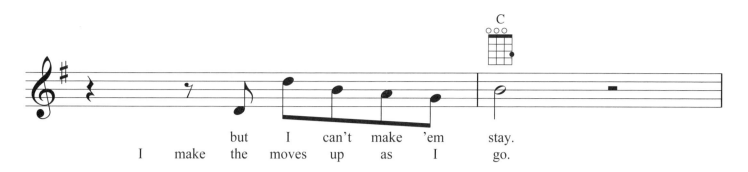

but I can't make 'em stay.
I make the moves up as I go.

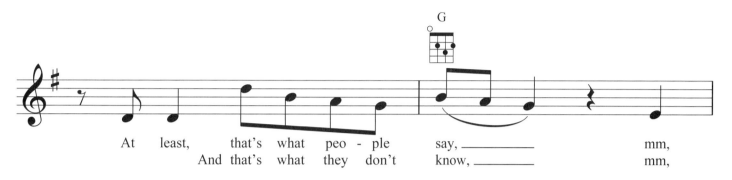

At least, that's what peo - ple say, _____ mm,
And that's what they don't know, _____ mm,

mm. That's what peo - ple say, _____ mm, mm. But I keep
mm. That's what they don't know, _____ mm, mm. But I keep

Pre-Chorus

cruis - ing; can't stop, won't stop mov - ing. } It's
cruis - ing; can't stop, won't stop groov - ing. }

like I got this mu - sic in my mind say - ing,

"It's gon - na be al - right." _____ 'Cause the

Chorus

play-ers gon-na play, play, play, play, play and the hat-ers gon-na hate, hate,

hate, hate, hate, ba-by. I'm just gon-na shake, shake, shake, shake, shake; _ I

shake it off, I shake it off. Heart - break-ers gon-na break, break,
(Ooh, _____ ooh!)

break, break, break and the fak-ers gon-na fake, fake, fake, fake, fake, ba-by.

To Coda

I'm just gon-na shake, shake, shake, shake, shake; _ I shake it off, I shake it

1. off. 2. I nev-er miss a
(Ooh, _____ ooh!)

2. off. (Ooh, _____ ooh!) I

Bridge

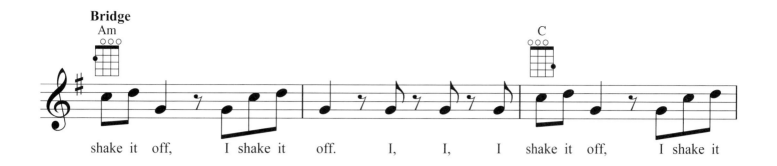

shake it off,   I shake it   off.   I,   I,   I   shake it off,   I shake it

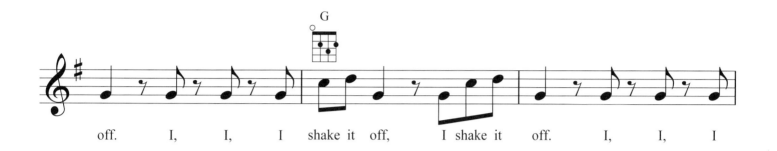

off.   I,   I,   I   shake it off,   I shake it   off.   I,   I,   I

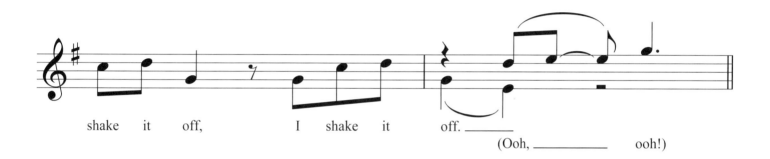

shake it off,   I shake it   off. _____   (Ooh, _____ ooh!)

Interlude

1. *Spoken: (See additional lyrics)*
2. *Rap: (See additional lyrics)*

D.S. al Coda

Rap ends   Yeah, _____   oh. _____ 'Cause the

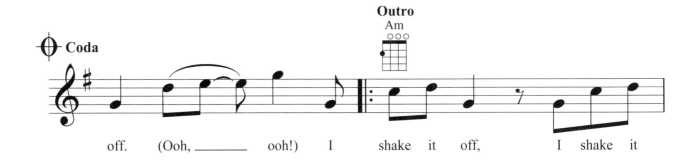

off. (Ooh, _____ ooh!) I shake it off, I shake it

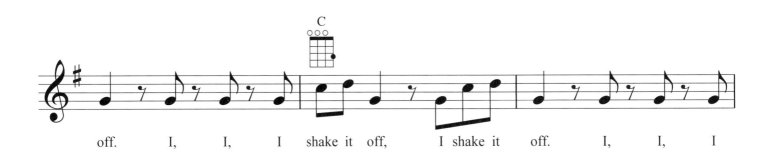

off. I, I, I shake it off, I shake it off. I, I, I

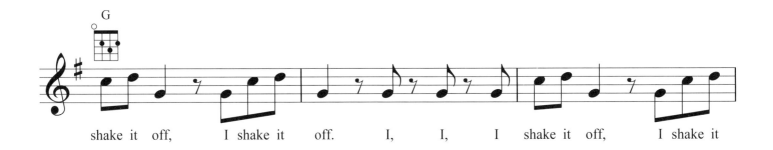

shake it off, I shake it off. I, I, I shake it off, I shake it

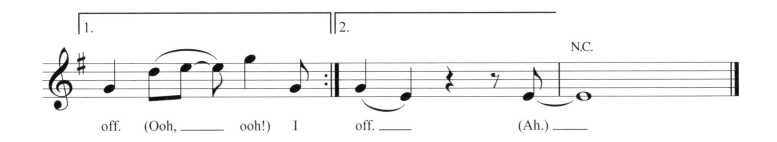

off. (Ooh, _____ ooh!) I off. _____ (Ah.) _____

Additional Lyrics

Spoken: Hey, hey, hey! Just think: While you've been gettin'
Down and out about the liars and the dirty, dirty cheats of the world,
You could've been gettin' down to this sick beat!

Rap: My ex-man brought his new girlfriend.
She's like, "Oh, my god!" But I'm just gonna shake.
And to the fella over there with the hella good hair,
Won't you come on over, baby? We can shake, shake, shake.

Our Song

Words and Music by Taylor Swift

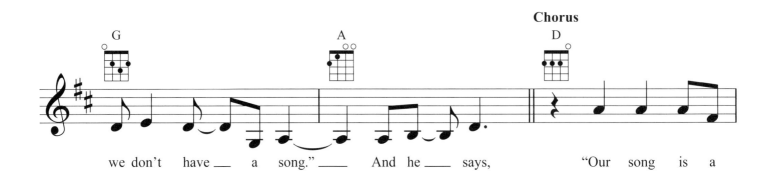

we don't have ___ a song." ___ And he ___ says, "Our song is a

slam - min' screen door, sneak - in' out late, tap - pin' on your win - dow,

when we're on the phone ___ and you talk real _____ slow 'cause it's

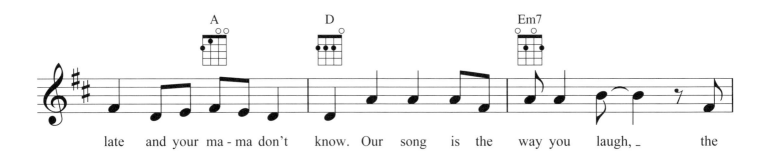

late and your ma - ma don't know. Our song is the way you laugh, _ the

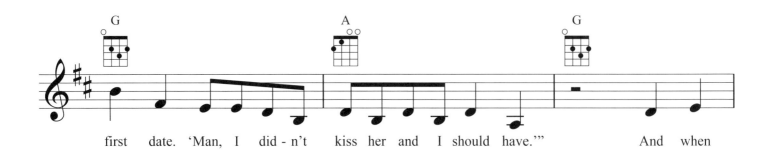

first date. 'Man, I did - n't kiss her and I should have.'" And when

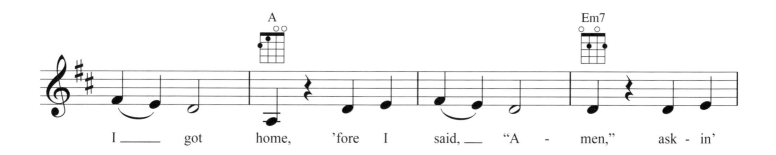

I ___ got home, 'fore I said, ___ "A - men," ask - in'

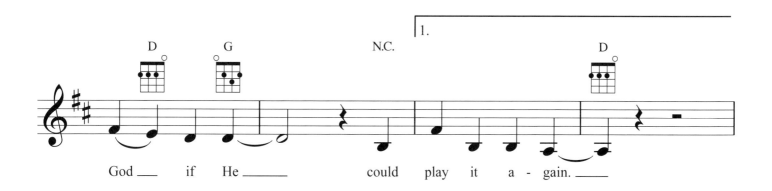

1.

God ___ if He ___ could play it a - gain. ___

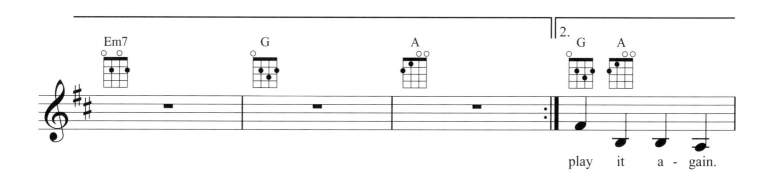

2.

play it a - gain.

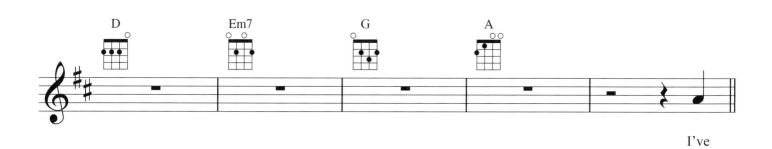

I've

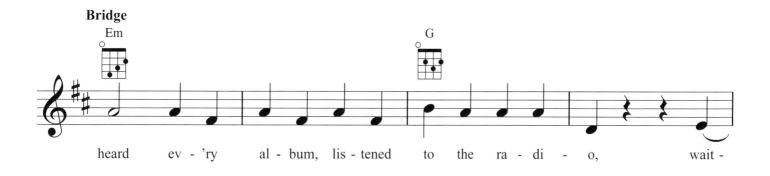

Bridge

heard ev - 'ry al - bum, lis - tened to the ra - di - o, wait -

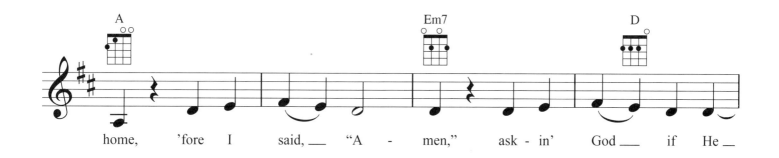

home, 'fore I said, __ "A - men," ask - in' God __ if He __

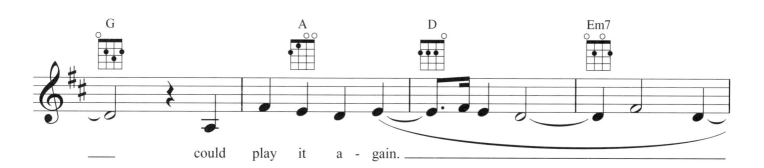

__ could play it a - gain. _____

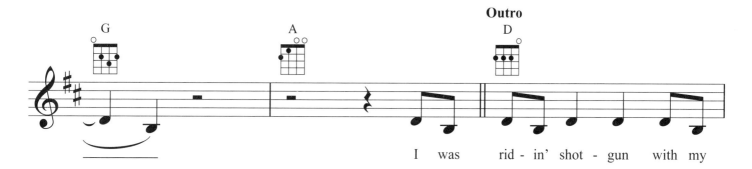

Outro

____ I was rid - in' shot - gun with my

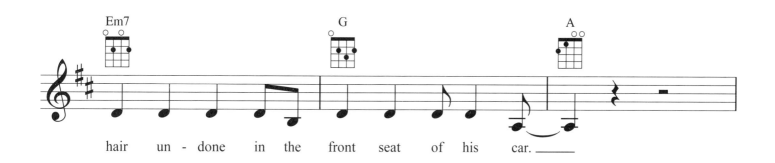

hair un - done in the front seat of his car. __

I grabbed a pen and an old nap - kin and I wrote down our ____ song.

Additional Lyrics

2. I was walkin' up the front porch after everything that day
   Had gone all wrong, had been trampled on and lost and thrown away.
   Got to the hallway, well on my way to my lovin' bed.
   I almost didn't notice all the roses and the note that said:

Sparks Fly

Words and Music by Taylor Swift

1. The way you move is like a full - on ___ rain - storm
2. *See additional lyrics*

and I'm a house _ of cards. ___ You're the kind of reck - less that should

send me run - ning, but I kind - a know _ that I won't get far. ___

And you stood _ there in front ___ of ___ me, ___ just close e - nough to touch, _

___ close e - nough to hope ___ you could - n't see _

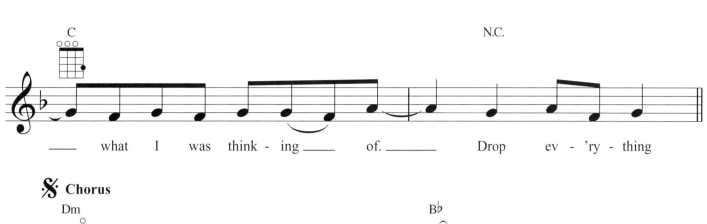

what I was think - ing _____ of. _____ Drop ev - 'ry - thing

𝄋 Chorus

now, _____ meet _____ me in the pour - ing rain. _____

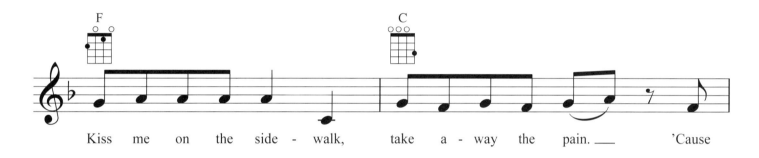

Kiss me on the side - walk, take a - way the pain. _____ 'Cause

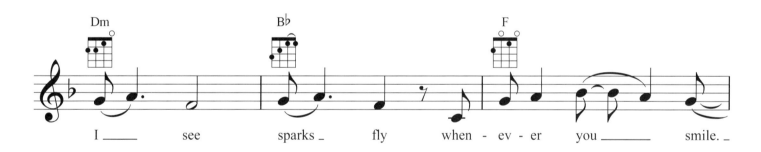

I _____ see sparks _ fly when - ev - er you _____ smile. _

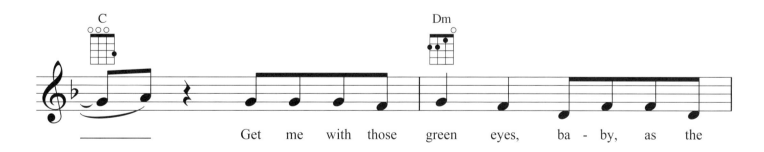

_____ Get me with those green eyes, ba - by, as the

lights go down. Give me some - thing that - 'll haunt me when _

To Coda

_____ you're not a - round. _____ 'Cause I _____ see

sparks _ fly when - ev - er you _____ smile. _

1.

2.

I'll

Bridge

run my fin - gers through _ your hair _ and watch _ the lights _ go _ wild. _

_____ Just keep on keep-ing your eyes _ on me. _ It's just

wrong e-nough to make it feel right. And
lead me up the stair - case. Won't you whis - per soft and slow?
I'm cap - ti - vat - ed by you, ba - by, like a

D.S. al Coda

Coda

fire - works show. Drop ev-'ry-thing

And the sparks fly.

Additional Lyrics

2. My mind forgets to remind me
   You're a bad idea.
   You touch me once and it's really something.
   You find I'm even better than you imagined I would be.
   I'm on my guard for the rest of the world,
   But with you, I know it's no good.
   And I could wait patiently,
   But I really wish you would...

Teardrops on My Guitar

Words and Music by Taylor Swift and Liz Rose

Today Was a Fairytale

from VALENTINE'S DAY
Words and Music by Taylor Swift

Additional Lyrics

3. Today was a fairytale.
   You've got a smile
   Takes me to another planet.
   Every move you make,
   Everything you say is right.
   Today was a fairytale.

4. Today was a fairytale.
   All that I can say
   Is now it's getting so much clearer.
   Nothing made sense
   Till the time I saw your face.
   Today was a fairytale.

We Are Never Ever Getting Back Together

Words and Music by Taylor Swift, Max Martin and Shellback

1. I re-mem-ber when we broke ___ up the first time,

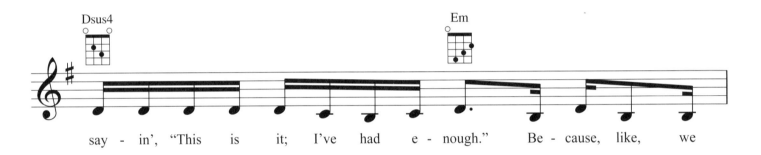

say-in', "This is it; I've had e-nough." Be-cause, like, we

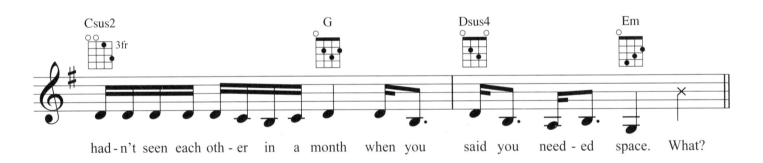

had-n't seen each oth-er in a month when you said you need-ed space. What?

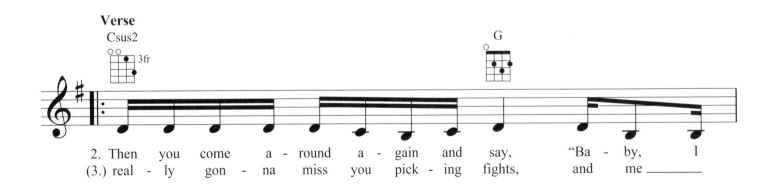

2. Then you come a-round a-gain and say, "Ba-by, I
(3.) real-ly gon-na miss you pick-ing fights, and me ___

miss you and I swear I'm gon - na change. Trust me." Re -
fall - ing for it, scream - ing that I'm right. And you would

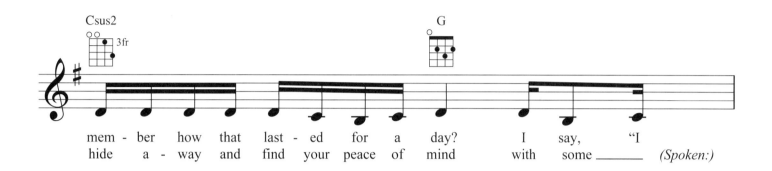

mem - ber how that last - ed for a day? I say, "I
hide a - way and find your peace of mind with some _____ *(Spoken:)*

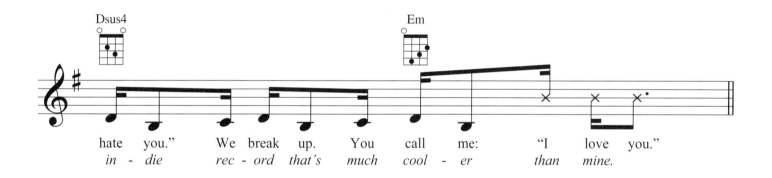

hate you." We break up. You call me: "I love you."
in - die rec - ord that's much cool - er than mine.

Pre-Chorus

Ooh, _____ ooh, ooh, __ we called it off a - gain __ last night. __ But
Ooh, _____ ooh, ooh, __ you called me up a - gain __ to - night. __ But

ooh, _____ ooh, ooh, __ this time __ I'm tell - ing you, I'm tell - ing you, }
ooh, _____ ooh, ooh, __ this time __ I'm tell - ing you, I'm tell - ing you, }

Chorus

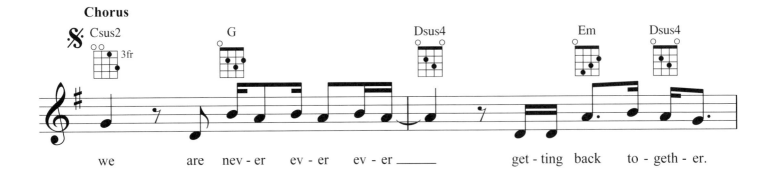

we are nev-er ev-er ev-er _____ get-ting back to-geth-er.

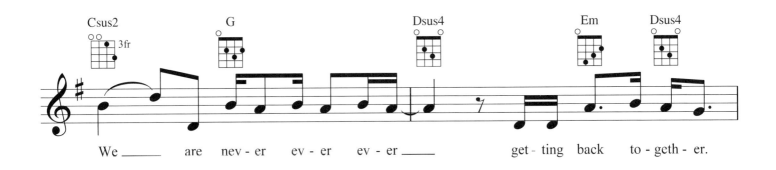

We _____ are nev-er ev-er ev-er _____ get-ting back to-geth-er.

You go talk to your ___ friends, talk to my _____ friends, talk to me. ___ But

To Coda

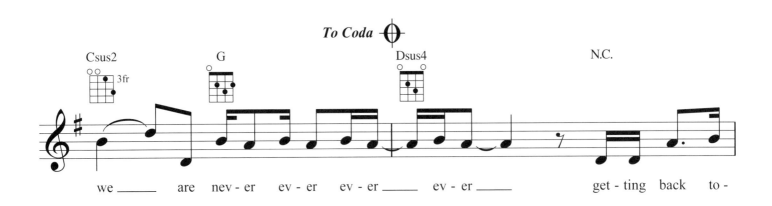

we _____ are nev-er ev-er ev-er _____ ev-er _____ get-ting back to-

geth-er, like ___ ev-er. 3. I'm

geth - er. _____ Ooh, _____ ooh, ooh. ___ Ooh, _____ ooh, ooh, ___ ooh,

ooh, _____ ooh, ooh. ___ Oh, oh, oh. _____

Bridge

I used to think ___ that we _____ were for - ev - er, ev - er, and

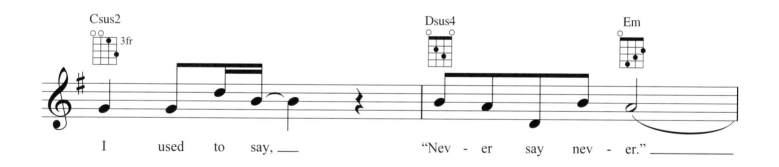

I used to say, ___ "Nev - er say nev - er." _____

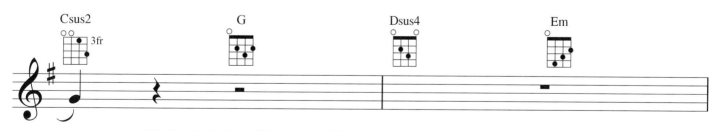

___ *(Spoken:) So he calls me up and he's like, "I still love you," and I'm like... I'm just... I mean,*

Willow

Words and Music by Taylor Swift and Aaron Dessner

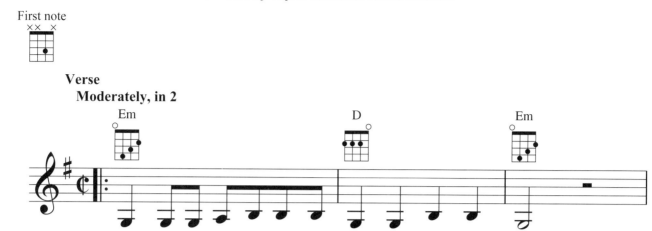

1. I'm like the wa-ter when your ship rolled in that night.
2. Life was a wil-low and it bent right to your wind.
3. Wait for the sig-nal and I'll meet you af-ter dark.

Rough on the sur-face, but you cut through like a
Head on the pil-low, I could feel you sneak-ing
Show me the plac-es where the oth-ers gave you

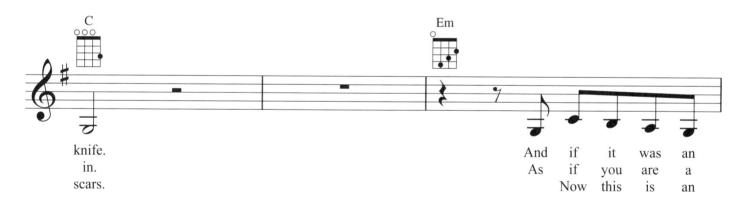

knife.
in.
scars.

And if it was an
As if you are a
Now this is an

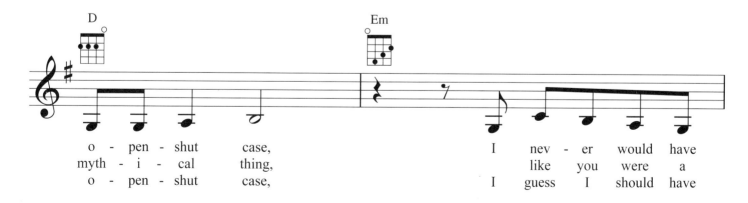

o-pen-shut case,
myth-i-cal thing,
o-pen-shut case,

I nev-er would have
like you were a
I guess I should have

known — from the look on your face. Lost in your
tro - phy or a cham - pi - on ring. And there was one
known from the look on your face. Ev - 'ry bait and

cur - rent like a price - less _____ wine.
prize ___ I'd ___ cheat to _____ win.
switch ___ was a work of _____ art.

Chorus 1

The more that you say, the less I

know. Wher - ev - er you stray, I fol - low. I'm beg - ging for

you to take my hand, wreck my plans. That's my

1.
man.

2., 3.
plans. That's my man. You know that my

Chorus 2

To Coda ⊕

train could take you home; an - y - where else is hol -

low. I'm beg - ging for you to take my hand, wreck my

plans. That's my man.

Bridge

Life was a wil - low and it bent right to your ___

1.

wind. ___ They count ___ me out

time and time a - gain.

White Horse

Words and Music by Taylor Swift and Liz Rose

First note

Verse
Moderately

1. Say you're sor - ry, that face ___ of an an - gel comes out ___
2. May - be I was na - ive, _____ got lost in your eyes and

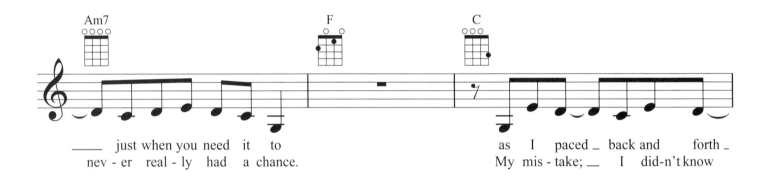

___ just when you need it to   as I paced ___ back and forth ___
nev - er real - ly had a chance.   My mis - take; ___ I did - n't know

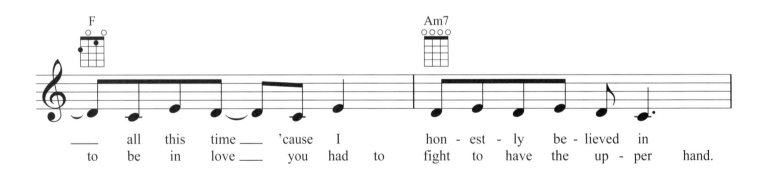

___ all this time ___ 'cause I   hon - est - ly be - lieved in
to be in love ___ you had to   fight to have the up - per hand.

you.   Hold - ing on, the days ___ drag on. Stu - pid girl, ___
I had   so man - y dreams a - bout you ___ and ___ me; ___ hap - py

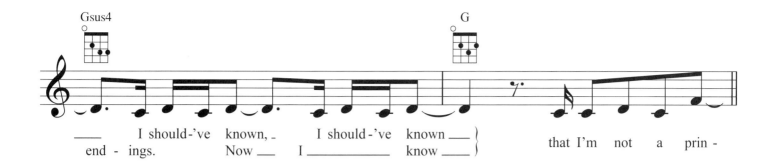

Gsus4   G

____ I should-'ve known, _ I should-'ve known ___ } that I'm not a prin-
end - ings. Now __ I _____ know ___ }

Chorus

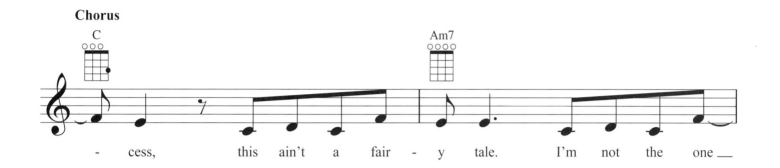

C   Am7

___ cess, this ain't a fair - y tale. I'm not the one __

F   Gsus4

___ you'll sweep off her feet, lead her up the stair - well. This ain't

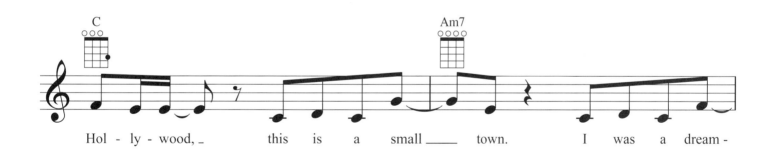

C   Am7

Hol - ly - wood, _ this is a small ____ town. I was a dream-

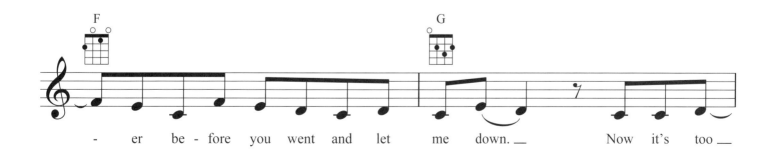

F   G

- er be - fore you went and let me down. _ Now it's too __

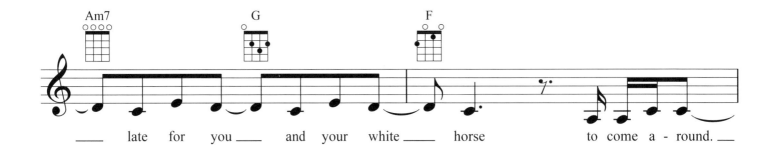

late for you ___ and your white ___ horse to come a - round. ___

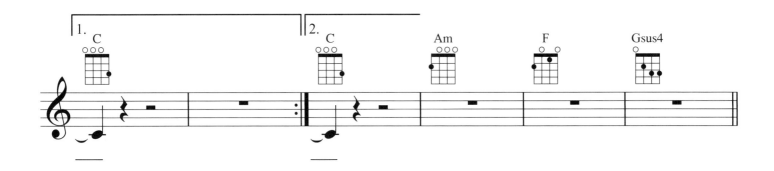

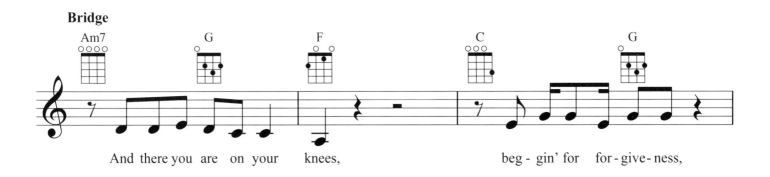

Bridge

And there you are on your knees, beg - gin' for for - give - ness,

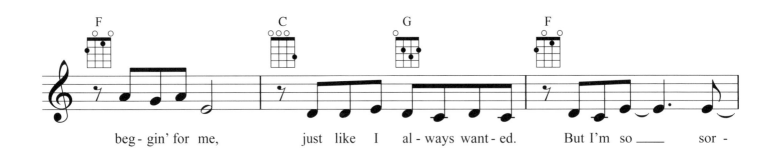

beg - gin' for me, just like I al - ways want - ed. But I'm so ___ sor -

Chorus

- ry. ___ 'Cause I'm not your prin - cess, this ain't a fair -

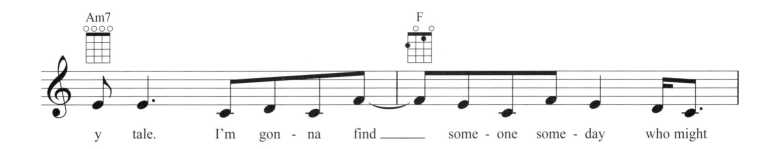

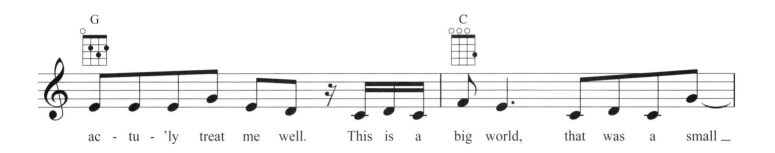

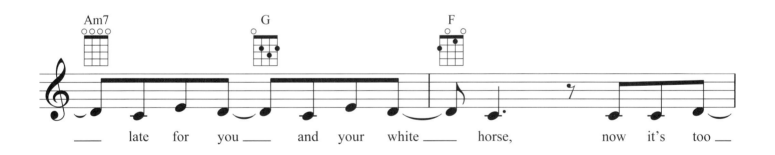

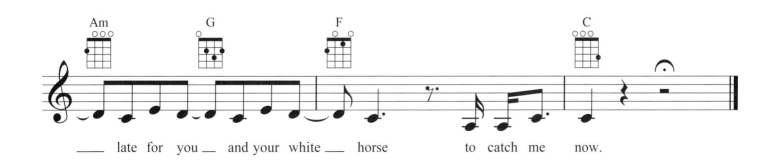

Wildest Dreams

Words and Music by Taylor Swift, Max Martin and Shellback

First note

Verse
Moderate Ballad, in 2

1. He said, "Let's get out of this town, drive out of the
(2.) "No one has to know what we do. His hands are in my

cit - y, a - way __ from the crowds." __ I thought, "Heav - en can't help me now." __
hair, __ his clothes are in my room. __ And his voice is a fa - mil - iar sound. __

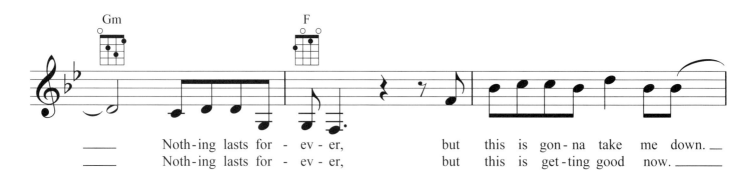

__ Noth - ing lasts for - ev - er, but this is gon - na take me down. __
__ Noth - ing lasts for - ev - er, but this is get - ting good now. __

__ He's so tall and hand - some as hell. He's so bad, but he
__ He's so tall and hand - some as hell. He's so bad, but he

does it so ___ well. _____ I can see the end ___ as it be - gins, my
does it so ___ well. _____ And when we've had our ver - y last kiss, my

%. Chorus

one con - di - tion ___ is: __ } Say you'll re - mem-ber me _____ stand-ing in a
last re - quest _ is: __ }

nice dress, star -ing at the sun -set, babe. Red lips and ros - y cheeks, _

___ say you'll see me a - gain, e - ven if it's just in your

wild - est dreams, _____ ah, _____ ah. _____

Wild - est dreams, _____ ah, _____

You Belong with Me

Words and Music by Taylor Swift and Liz Rose